Also by Shirley O. Corriher

CookWise
BakeWise

KitchenWise

Essential Food Science
for Home Cooks

Shirley O. Corriher

SCRIBNER

New York London Toronto Sydney New Delhi

Scribner
An Imprint of Simon & Schuster, Inc.
1230 Avenue of the Americas
New York, NY 10020

First Scribner hardcover edition November 2020

SCRIBNER and design are registered trademarks of The Gale Group, Inc.,
used under license by Simon & Schuster, Inc., the publisher of this work.

For information about special discounts for bulk purchases,
please contact Simon & Schuster Special Sales at 1-866-506-1949
or business@simonandschuster.com.

The Simon & Schuster Speakers Bureau can bring authors to your live event.
For more information or to book an event, contact the Simon & Schuster Speakers
Bureau at 1-866-248-3049 or visit our website at www.simonspeakers.com.

Interior design by Erich Hobbing

Manufactured in the United States of America

1   3   5   7   9   10   8   6   4   2

Library of Congress Cataloging-in-Publication Data has been applied for.

ISBN 978-1-9821-4068-7
ISBN 978-1-9821-4069-4 (ebook)

To everyone who has wondered why

CONTENTS

INTRODUCTION

I was a research biochemist for the Vanderbilt University School of Medicine before my former husband and I opened a boys school together, and there I began my culinary adventures. We started with two boys but had over thirty within a year, and I did all the cooking for the students and staff, three meals a day, seven days a week. We grew to 148 (including teachers). For eleven years, I got heavy-duty, hands-on cooking experience. I planned the meals, bought the groceries, and cooked. Kitchen staff was hard to find because the school was so isolated on the bluffs of the Chattahoochee River, so I was mostly on my own.

Desperate for help, I pored over cookbooks. To my dismay, many recipes from "good" cookbooks did not work, or produced miserable food! I did not want to waste expensive ingredients and my time on miserable food. I knew how to do research from my chemistry days, so I went to the science literature, found an expert, picked up the phone, and made a call. If I had a problem with fruits and vegetables, I called Dr. Robert Shewfelt, professor of food science and technology at the University of Georgia. For a starch problem, I called Dr. Carl Hoseney, professor of grain science at Kansas State University. These experts were generous with their time and knowledge, and were an enormous help to my education. Over the years I studied with culinary experts from all over, including those from La Varenne and Le Cordon Bleu in Paris, and Leiths School of Food and Wine in London.

Eventually, I developed a reputation for being able to solve cooking problems. Teachers; chefs; food producers like Pillsbury, Procter & Gamble, etc.; and my hero, Julia Child, consulted with me about their issues in the kitchen. I loved Julia. She would call the next day and tell me exactly what she did and how it came out. With big companies, I wouldn't know whether what I suggested had worked until one of their people would rush up to me at a conference and say, "You saved us on that chocolate cake!"

I have taught all over the United States and from Vancouver to Melbourne to Erice, in Sicily. I love to share my findings, so I have written three books: *CookWise* (which won a James Beard award in 1998), *BakeWise* (which won a James Beard award in 2008), and now *KitchenWise*, a handy guide to food science with a few of my favorite recipes so that you can create magnificent food.

A little science can free you to be much more creative in the kitchen. For example, 1 egg will almost set 1 cup of liquid. For a quiche or custard with 2 cups of cream or milk, for a firm set, you will need 3 eggs, or 2 eggs plus 2 yolks. Now that you know the limiting factor, you are free to go wild with the rest of the recipe—add all the veggies, cheese, or bacon you like!

KitchenWise's goals are to enable you to spot bad recipes and know how to fix them, to know some science of taste and flavor so you can make a good dish taste great, and to allow you to consistently prepare wonderful, delicious, beautiful food. *Bon appétit!*

CHAPTER ONE

FLAVOR

WHAT MAKES FOOD TASTE GREAT

For centuries, cooks have strived to make the most flavorful dishes. By learning more about taste and flavor, we can make good food taste great.

What Is the Difference Between Taste and Flavor?

We tend to use the words "taste" and "flavor" interchangeably, but scientifically speaking, they're not the same. The physical taste receptors on our tongues and in our mouths correspond to only five primary tastes: sweet, sour, salty, bitter, and the savory sensation called umami. Taste buds contain clusters of fifty to one hundred receptor cells that represent all five tastes. While some areas are more sensitive to certain tastes, we actually have receptors for all five tastes on all areas of the tongue.

Technically, taste refers only to these five physical taste receptors, while flavor includes all the things—taste, temperature, texture, aroma, color—that help us recognize a food as being herby, nutty, spicy, fruity, and so on. Aroma is key to identifying these flavors, as our sense of smell is much more refined than our sense of taste.

1

Flavor includes everything that contributes to our thinking a food is delicious.

The Role of Taste Receptors

Taste receptors can help sustain life. To our bodies, sweet indicates energy-producing sugars, bitter is a warning of possible toxins (deadly alkaloids are bitter), salty points to minerals that our bodies cannot survive without, and umami indicates life-giving protein.

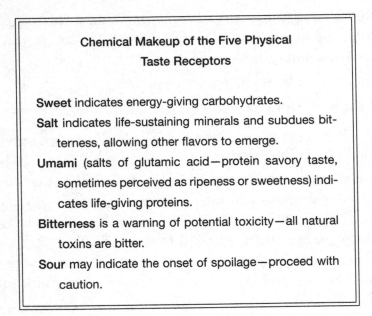

Chemical Makeup of the Five Physical Taste Receptors

Sweet indicates energy-giving carbohydrates.

Salt indicates life-sustaining minerals and subdues bitterness, allowing other flavors to emerge.

Umami (salts of glutamic acid—protein savory taste, sometimes perceived as ripeness or sweetness) indicates life-giving proteins.

Bitterness is a warning of potential toxicity—all natural toxins are bitter.

Sour may indicate the onset of spoilage—proceed with caution.

What Sends Taste Buds Zinging?

Dr. Harold McGee, author of *On Food and Cooking*, points out that big food compounds like carbohydrates, proteins, and fats do not affect our taste buds much, but their smaller component parts—sugars from carbohydrates, amino acids from proteins, and fatty acids from fats—are extremely flavorful. This is exactly what some of our basic tastes indicate. For example, sugars set off our sweet taste buds, and certain amino acids and small pieces of protein set off our umami taste buds.

How do we make these small flavorful compounds that send our taste buds "zinging"? Cooks use everything from heat (actual cooking) to the interaction of ingredients to techniques like layering (adding ingredients at different stages of cooking) to creating umami by selecting the right ingredients (choosing ripe products or fermented products for an intensely flavorful result) to strategically storing food (aging and standing, allowing the breakdown of food [carbohydrates to sugars, protein to amino acids, and fats to fatty acids] for more flavor) to get great flavors.

HEAT FOR FLAVOR

We humans and our ancestors owe much to cooking with heat—we actually owe the size of our brains to cooking. Harvard's Dr. Richard Wrangham and his colleagues studied how important cooking was in human evolution. Cooking made plant foods softer and easier to chew and substantially increased their available energy, particularly in the case of starchy tubers. This enabled *Homo erectus* to evolve with larger brains. Bigger brains required more food. The modern human brain requires a whopping 20 to 25 percent of our energy (food) intake!

When we apply heat to food, the flavor changes as structures break down. These physical changes make more nutrients available to our bodies, and also make more flavors available. Many vegetables, like onions, carrots, sweet peppers, and fennel, seem to become sweeter when cooked. There are several factors at work behind this phenomenon, including evaporation and chemical changes that remove some acidic or unpleasant-tasting compounds.

Why do carrots get "sweeter" when cooked? The actual weight or percentage of sugar in raw carrots and cooked carrots is the same. But when heated, some of the molecules of double sugars (glucose) break down into single sugars (fructose), which magnifies sweetness.

Increased sweetness with cooking can be as simple as cell destruction. The sugars are in the carrots all along, but in raw carrots the cell structure is so firm and rigid that even chewing does not liberate many of those sugars. The cell structure of carrots is destroyed by cooking, making their sugars easily accessible.

Many flavor changes take place when we heat food—everything from the structural breakdown just described to water loss to removal of off-tasting compounds.

Heat and Water Loss

When water is lost, flavors become more intense. This happens with a small water loss, as in a brief steaming or boiling of vegetables, or an extensive water loss, as in drying. You can get marvelous, intense flavors by oven-drying tomatoes at 200°F for an hour or two. Cooks seeking lots of flavor with a minimum of ingredients will oven-dry seedless grapes, which become sweet, complex flavor enhancers.

In roasting, the liquid that comes out of the vegetable cells as they are heated immediately evaporates, and this drying concentrates flavor. Long roasting of vegetables like onions and root vegetables caramelizes their exterior for more complex, sweet tastes (for more on caramelization, see the following section, "Browning").

Heat and Loss (or Formation) of Unpleasant Flavors

Two families of vegetables whose flavors change dramatically with cooking are onions and members of the genus *Brassica*. When onions cook, some of their strong sulfur compounds dissolve or break down, and many evaporate, making the onions milder and more pleasant or sweeter-tasting.

Members of the brassica family (cabbage, cauliflower, broccoli, Brussels sprouts, kale, mustard, rutabagas, collards, turnips, etc.) do not fare well flavor-wise with extended cooking. If you increase the cooking time of cabbage from five to seven minutes, you double the quantity of pungent hydrogen sulfide gas (which has the smell of rotten eggs) the cabbage produces, whereas cabbage cooked briefly has fascinating, subtle, sweet flavors.

Flavor In/Flavor Out

Most of the time, cooks want to keep the flavor and nutrients in vegetables. Classic cooking methods like blanching (plunging a vegetable into boiling water for a brief cooking time), steaming, broiling, grilling, or stir-frying do an excellent job of keeping flavors in. Chemically, the outer starch cells swell to limit flavor loss. High-temperature cooking like grilling and frying can produce browning reactions (see the following section, "Browning"), which add to and enhance flavors in a major way.

Sometimes cooks want to extract flavors, such as when

making stocks or sauces. They do this by putting foods into cold water, bringing the temperature up slowly, and simmering for a long time. If you have ever sampled the onions or celery that are strained out after making stock, you know they are almost tasteless, having given all their flavor to the broth.

Browning

When table sugar (sucrose) reaches very high temperatures (over 300°F), it melts, then starts to break down, or caramelize. Different sugars are formed, sugars break apart, some of these rejoin. At any given moment between clear melted sugar and dark caramel, there is a unique mixture of sugars—over 128 different sugars have been identified. Many of these are shades of brown and have the wonderful flavors we associate with caramel.

There is a way to make the delicious sweet compounds that you get in caramelization at lower temperatures. The Maillard reaction is a series of complex reactions that produce, at much lower temperatures, the same sweet compounds that you get in caramel, plus many others, because, in addition to sugars, proteins are involved. Everything from toast to fried foods and roasts get this rich-tasting brown coating from the complex reactions caused when certain sugars and proteins are exposed to heat.

Three conditions are necessary for successful lower-temperature browning: proteins, certain sugars (known as reducing sugars), and a nonacidic environment (acids prevent browning). But with low acidity, the more reducing sugars (sugars with a certain shape) and protein in a product, the browner and more flavorful it gets.

Some sugars, like glucose (found in corn syrup), enhance browning. If you substitute as little as one tablespoon of corn syrup for one tablespoon of sugar in a cookie recipe, you will get cookies with a remarkably browner surface. If you baste a turkey or roast a chicken with something that has reducing sugars and protein, it will get much browner than if you basted it with oil.

Browning meat at the end of cooking instead of at the beginning produces fast browning. Because juices containing protein and sugar have come to the surface and evaporated at the end of the cooking time, there is a considerably greater concentration of surface sugar and protein. Now, with an elevated temperature, browning occurs rapidly.

Cooks use these delicious sugars and breakdown products from browning and caramelization to enhance flavors in all kinds of dishes. For example, when reducing a sauce, some of the sauce dries on the sides of the pan and caramelizes with the heat. Good cooks carefully redissolve these bits into the sauce. Browning can happen suddenly. Care should be taken not to over brown, as too much browning can taste burnt and may also be less healthy.

HOW INGREDIENT INTERACTIONS INCREASE FLAVOR

Salt

Salt has complex, indirect influences on flavor. Pastry chefs have always said adding a pinch of salt to desserts brings out their sweetness. Dr. Gary Beauchamp and researchers at the Monell Chemical Senses Center in Philadelphia demonstrated the interplay between salt and sweetness in a study. Beauchamp had a diagram representing bitterness in a dish. When sugar was added, the bitterness dropped significantly, so that sweetness and bitterness were equal in strength. Next, he added a little salt. The bitterness dropped to nothing and there was only sweetness left.

To re-create this at home, get some tonic water, which contains both bitter quinine and sugar to moderate it. Pour two samples of the tonic water. Taste one plain; to the second sample, add a pinch of salt, then taste it. Amazingly, you will find the bitterness dramatically reduced—the sample is almost like sugar water!

You have probably experienced this many times, when you think about it. It's why some people put salt on grapefruit or cantaloupe.

Sugar

Researchers at the University of Nottingham in England have analyzed the gases present in the nasal cavity. They gave test subjects gum that contained mint and sugar and asked them to chew until the flavor was gone. When subjects reported the flavor was gone, there was still mint in their nasal cavities. They were given a dose of sugar, and the mint flavor returned. A friend from the UK reports that as a child, when their gum ran out of flavor, they rolled it in the family sugar dish and it was like new.

As little as a half teaspoon of sugar in a dish can make an amazing taste difference.

• • •

Flavor

Here is a recipe for a delicious, refreshing salad that illustrates the effects of salt and sugar on flavor.

PEA SALAD

What This Recipe Shows

A small amount of salt suppresses the onion's bitterness to allow other flavors to come through.

The addition of sugar to this dressing changes an ordinary salad into an extraordinary salad.

---

1 head washed iceberg or butter lettuce chopped
    or torn into ½- to ¾-inch pieces, drained well
½ large red onion, chopped medium fine
3 stalks celery, chopped medium fine
1 (16-ounce) package frozen green peas
¼ cup mayonnaise
¼ cup sour cream
1 teaspoon sugar
¼ teaspoon fine sea salt
4 strips crisp cooked bacon, crumbled (optional)

In a glass bowl, sprinkle lettuce first, then chopped onion, celery, and defrosted green peas.

In a small bowl, stir together mayonnaise, sour cream, sugar, and salt. Toss this mayonnaise mixture with the other ingredients. Low-fat mayonnaise and low-fat sour cream are also delicious in this recipe.

Sprinkle with bacon crumbs and serve cold.

Makes 6 servings

Intensely Flavored Ingredients

Good cooks keep an arsenal of ingredients on hand to add kick to their recipes.

Citrus Zest

Citrus zest (finely grated orange peel, lemon peel, lime peel, etc.) adds a real flavor burst to a dish.

Fresh Ginger

Grated fresh ginger is another intense flavoring ingredient. Remember, fresh ginger contains an enzyme that will attack collagen (the casing of meat fibers and a main component of connective tissue) and meat fibers. It will prevent gelatin (which is what collagen turns into when it's cooked for longer times at lower temperatures, as in braising, for example) from setting. Ginger tenderizes meat, which is why it is mixed with thinly sliced chicken or beef and allowed to stand briefly before the meat is cooked.

Fermented Foods

During fermentation, large, bland molecules break down into smaller, more flavorful compounds, producing dramatic changes in flavor. Fermented products—including wine, coffee, tea, and soy sauce, to name a few—can add complex flavors.

FLAVORFUL FAT

Some flavor components in foods dissolve in water, and some dissolve in fat. One of the reasons fat-free foods often taste so boring is that the fat-soluble flavors in the dish remain locked in the food. Even a tiny bit of fat can dissolve and carry flavors, making a dish that contains some fat much more flavorful than if it were fat-free. Fat dissolves and releases fat-soluble flavors that might otherwise be locked up. Cooks know that fat makes food taste better by coating the mouth and holding flavors for complete and rounded tastes.

LAYERING FOR FLAVOR ENHANCEMENT

Cooks "layer" flavors for complexity of both texture and taste. Famed Creole chef Paul Prudhomme sautéed onions, peppers, and celery at the beginning of a gumbo, then added fresh onions, peppers, and celery halfway through cooking and again shortly before finishing. The ones added at the first instance cook to a mush, while those added last are crisp-cooked, and those added halfway have a texture in between. Each batch contributes different flavors and textures.

THE MAGIC OF UMAMI

Have you ever wondered why people put ketchup on hamburgers, or why pizza is so popular? It's all about umami, our fifth taste receptor, and synergism—the interaction of two or more substances that produces a combined effect greater than the sum of their parts. When you combine one source of umami with another type of umami, you don't get double the taste kick—you get *eight times* the flavor. Wow!

Descriptions of this just-short-of-undefinable taste can range from "meaty" or "savory" to "yummy," "tasty," "delicious," or "absolute perfection." I first heard the word "umami" years ago, when it was used by Jon Rowley, a fish expert, as a description of "indescribably delicious"—a perfection in taste that sends one into a state of ecstasy.

Taste researchers Stephen D. Roper and Nirupa Chaudhari of the University of Miami Miller School of Medicine brought this near mystical taste to an earthly level in 1997 when they identified taste buds on the tongue that respond to umami, and have now cloned umami taste receptors. This put umami on a firmer footing than some of our long-recognized tastes. The receptors for sour and salty are well understood, but there is still controversy about bitter, and sweet appears to have multiple mechanisms.

Sources of Umami

"Yummy" and "tasty" sound great, but exactly how do cooks accomplish them in their dishes? The umami taste is produced by a number of naturally occurring compounds—salts of amino acids like glutamic acid, and nucleotides like guanosine 5'-monophosphate (GMP), inosine 5'-monophosphate (IMP), and adenosine 5'-monophosphate (AMP).

Let me translate. Amino acids are the basic units that link together to form proteins. Proteins can consist of hundreds of amino acids hooked together. Nucleotides are small molecules used in protein synthesis as part of the template to tell which amino acids are joined to form a specific protein. The important thing to know is that these are small flavorful molecules, not huge proteins.

Synergism

Some umami taste–producing compounds have a magnifying effect on each other. A mixture of 50 percent glutamate and 50 percent umami nucleotide produces eight times the flavor as either of the umami compounds alone.

For maximum flavor, use a natural source of glutamate and a nucleotide source of umami. Some chefs keep dried shiitake mushroom powder, which is available from a number of sources, on hand to sprinkle on dishes for super umami flavor.

Selected Natural Sources Of Umami-Rich Foods**	
Natural Sources of Glutamate (amino acid)	
Food	(mg/100 g)
Kombu (rausu, ma, rishiri, hidako, naga)*	240–3380
Parmigiano Reggiano, Italy (hard type)	1200–1680
Soy sauce	400–1700
Nori	550–1350
Dried tomatoes	650–1140
Dried shiitake mushrooms	1060
Nam pla	950
Oyster sauce	900
Miso	200–700
Anchovies	630
Salted squid	620
Green tea	220–670
Dry-cured hams	340
Emmental cheese	310
Kimchi	240
Clam	210
Cheddar cheese	180
Oyster	40–150
Scallop, natto*	140
Shimeji mushroom	140
Shrimp/prawn	120
Green peas, lotus root, garlic, mussel*	100–110
Corn	70–110
Common mushroom	40–110
Uni (Sea Urchin)	100

Natural Sources of Glutamate (amino acid)	
Food	**(mg/100 g)**
Potatoes	30–100
Enoki mushroom	90
Japanese littleneck clam	90
Chinese cabbage	40–90
Bamboo shoots	14–90
Caviar, shungiku*	80
Soy beans, fava beans*	60–80
Sweet potato, spinach, truffles, carrot*	40–80
Shiitake mushroom	70
Daikon	30–70
Niboshi, kotsuobushi*	30–50
Asparagus, cabbage*	30–50
Chicken	20–50
Onion, green onion*	20–50
Wakame	2–50
Frozen shelled shrimp	15–30
Celery, octopus*	20–30
Mackerel, sardine*	10–30
Chicken eggs	20
Burdock root, ginger*	20
Natural Sources of Guanylate (nucleotide)	
Food	**(mg/100 g)**
Dried shiitake mushrooms	150
Enoki mushrooms	50 (heated)
Nori	3–80
Dried tomatoes	10

Natural Sources of Inosinate (nucleotide)	
Food	(mg/100 g)
Niboshi (dried baby sardines)	350–800
Kotsuobushi (dried, fermented, smoked Skipjack tuna)	470–700
Tuna	250–360
Aji (horse mackerel)	270–330
Sea bream	180–300
Hamachi (fish)	230–290
Sawara (Spanish mackerel)	250–280
Mackerel	130–280
Sardine	280
Bonito	130–270
Dried shirasu (whitebait)	240
Chicken	150–230
Pork	230
Cod	180
Shrimp/prawn	90
Beef	80
Oyster	20

* Foods with similar or the same values are listed together to save space.
** Courtesy of the Umami Information Center. Copyright Umami Information Center

THE BEST HAMBURGER STEAKS

When my children were growing up, this was their favorite dinner. These burgers are a perfect example of the synergism of umami at work. Tomatoes (in the ketchup) are a source of a glutamate and beef is a source of a nucleotide. *Wham!* Eight times the flavor! No need for buns.

What This Recipe Shows

Salt reduces bitterness to enhance flavors in other ingredients.

Heating the empty pan prevents sticking.

1½ pounds ground beef (any kind is fine—my favorite is ground chuck)
1 cup thinly sliced mushrooms (optional)
½ teaspoon fine sea salt
Ground black pepper
½ cup ketchup
½ cup water

Divide the ground beef into 4 equal portions and shape them into round patties 3 to 4 inches in diameter.

Heat a large skillet (10 to 12 inches, large enough to hold all 4 patties) over medium heat until its upper edge is hot. Increase the heat a little and add the patties. Cook until well browned on the bottom, about 3 minutes. Turn the patties over and cook until browned on the other side.

Drain off as much fat from the skillet as you can. Off the heat, add the mushrooms, sprinkle with the salt and pepper to taste, and stir.

Return the skillet to the heat, add the ketchup and water, and stir. Simmer until the sauce has reduced and the meat is cooked thoroughly, about 3 minutes. Spoon the sauce over the patties and serve hot.

Makes 4 servings

SELECTING THE MOST FLAVORFUL INGREDIENTS

When you taste a truly ripe piece of fruit, you experience umami. As tomatoes ripen, there are changes in glutamate, a compound that stimulates your umami taste receptors. The glutamate in a tomato goes from 10 mg per 100 ml of juice to 100 mg per 100 ml. This dramatic change is reflected in its taste—from a cardboard-tasting, unripe tomato to the absolutely delicious flavors in a truly ripe tomato.

In ripening, like in fermentation or aging, a wild mix of reactions and changes takes place. Fruits go from a hard, sour, inedible, almost-invisible by-product of a plant to a sweet, juicy object with brilliant colors and enticing aromas. They change in color, taste, aroma, size, weight, texture, and nutrient content.

A plant needs distribution of its seeds. If all the seeds fall directly under the plant, as they grow they will rob each other of nutrients and light. So the plant makes fruit, the plant's seed-bearing ovary, enticing to animals, that will eat the fruit and spread the seeds within it. To attract the attention of animals, the fruit becomes bright in color, large, aromatic, and sweet. Humans should look for the same qualities and choose the brightest and most fragrant options on hand.

STORING UP FLAVOR

The breakdown of proteins during aging and ripening produces flavorful amino acids. Certain foods, like the great cheese Parmigiano Reggiano, get their intense flavors from breakdowns that occur during long storage, when some of their proteins break down into amino acids. The shiny flakes in aged Parmesan are crystallized tyrosine—the amino acid that is supposed to pep you up. I once saw a shop owner in a tiny Italian village who was making use of this fact for promotional purposes. In his small cheese shop window, he had a large sign that read, "Parmigiano Reggiano is more effective than Viagra!"

ALCOHOL AND FLAVOR

Alcohol, be it wine, beer, or hard liquor like vodka, is a powerful flavor extractor. It dissolves not only water-soluble and fat-soluble flavors but also dissolves flavor components that neither water nor fat can dissolve. For example, we use alcohol to extract flavor from vanilla beans, and the reward is vanilla extract.

This ability of alcohol to extract and carry flavors makes it a great asset for cooks. For hundreds of years, chefs have used wine to deglaze pans. When you splash a few tablespoons of wine into a skillet that was used to sauté meat or vegetables, you usually scrape up the stuck-on bits of food so they'll dissolve in the wine, a technique known as deglazing the pan. By doing this, you're not only getting the flavors of the wine and of the caramelized bits in your dish, you're also getting some extra flavors that only alcohol can extract. However, wine is not the only thing that can be used to deglaze a pan.

Mixtures of water, fat, and/or alcohol dissolve and carry more flavor components than one of these alone. Some things dissolve in water, some in fat, and some in alcohol. Alcohol, however, has the great advantage that it dissolves both fat and water-soluble components, as well as some flavor components that neither fat nor water can dissolve.

Cooks know that a small amount of alcohol can make a huge flavor difference. Cookbook author and teacher Patricia Wells once asked me why a little vodka, which is relatively weak in flavor but high in alcohol, made such a difference in the taste of tomato sauces. Vodka itself does not have a lot of taste, and the tomato sauce is frequently boiled for ten minutes or more after the vodka is added, long enough to boil off most of the alcohol. But there are flavor components in tomatoes that are alcohol soluble. Once the alcohol dissolves that flavor component and releases it into the sauce, it doesn't matter what happens to the alcohol. It has done its job.

That teaspoon or tablespoon of sherry added to the soup may not seem like much, but it can mean a lot flavor-wise!

Does It All Evaporate?

Alcohol boils at a lower temperature than water in the tomato sauce, for example, so you'd think the alcohol would completely evaporate before the water, but this doesn't happen. Some of the alcohol and water combine to form an inseparable mixture called an azeotrope. Even after lengthy boiling, some alcohol remains bound with water.

Not surprisingly, the cooking method and cooking time also influence how much alcohol evaporates. Flambéing removes about 25 percent of the original alcohol. Simmering on the stovetop for 30 minutes evaporates about 65 percent of the alcohol, and 2½ hours of simmering removes about 95 percent of the alcohol.

One Bite Influences the Next

The taste of one bite or sip influences the taste of the next bite or sip. This is clear in tasting wine. Food changes the way wine tastes. The dominant taste in the food changes the flavor of the wines, in varying degrees.

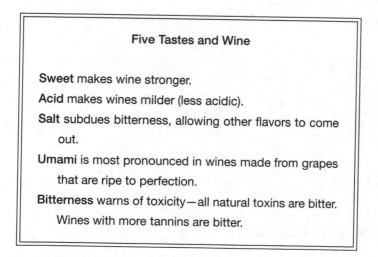

Five Tastes and Wine

Sweet makes wine stronger.

Acid makes wines milder (less acidic).

Salt subdues bitterness, allowing other flavors to come out.

Umami is most pronounced in wines made from grapes that are ripe to perfection.

Bitterness warns of toxicity—all natural toxins are bitter. Wines with more tannins are bitter.

CHAPTER TWO

PROTEINS

Proteins, whether they be in the form of animal muscle fiber (beef, pork, lamb, chicken, turkey, etc.), or other proteins such as fish, eggs, and cheese, are a major part of our diet. Knowing how to cook proteins so that they are moist, tender, and flavorful can improve meals, and knowing how to solve protein cooking problems can save time and money.

HOW PROTEINS COOK

Natural raw proteins are totally separate, individual units. Think of them as pieces of ribbon, curled around or wadded up. They have bonds across their curls to hold them together, with plenty of room for light to go between them. You can see right through a raw egg white.

Coagulation Through Heat

When you heat many natural proteins, or expose them to acids, salts, or even to air, the bonds holding them together break down. The springs and coils pop open and unwind. This unwound protein (called a denatured protein, because it has changed from its natural form) is now floating about with its bonds sticking out. Immediately, it runs into another unwound protein that has its bonds exposed, and the two join. Now there is no longer room for light to go between the proteins. The egg white becomes opaque, solid white; the chicken breast or fish becomes solid white. The proteins have coagulated (cooked).

When proteins from different directions join together in a great three-dimensional mesh, water is trapped throughout. This cooked protein is soft and moist and tender, like a perfectly cooked, juicy chicken breast. If you continue to heat the proteins, or expose them to acid, the bonds between the proteins tighten up and squeeze the water out. The proteins then become tough and dry.

The big secret in protein cookery is gently, gently. You want just enough heat or acid or exposure to air to make the proteins denature (unwind) and loosely join together.

The degree of cooking of a tender, lean cut of beef is in part a matter of personal preference. From the technical point of view, the meat proteins start to lose a little moisture when their temperature reaches as low as 105°F, when the meat shrinks around the fiber bundles the protein mesh tightens. Around 140°F, the meat fibers start to shrink lengthwise, and real moisture loss and toughening begin. Tender, lean cuts of beef are usually very juicy if kept at 145°F.

Time and Temperature

Different proteins coagulate (cook) at different temperatures, and even the same protein can cook at different temperatures. Usually it is a matter of both time and temperature. With a stirred custard (crème anglaise), for instance, if you heat the custard slowly (in a double boiler or over simmering water with constant stirring), it starts to thicken when heated to around 160°F and gets to a good "coat your spoon" thickness between 170°F and 179°F. At this thickness, you can take it off the heat and cool it. Eggs in the custard cook to hard curds at 180°F, and if you get to this temperature too quickly, you will have a thin liquid with bits of scrambled eggs floating about instead of a thick, smooth custard. Heating custard slowly, you have a ten- to twelve-degree temperature range from the moment it thickens until it turns into scrambled eggs, giving you time to get it off the heat safely after it begins to thicken.

However, if you heat the same custard over direct high heat, the custard does not start to thicken around 160°F. It does not even begin to thicken until it reaches 179°F. You have only one degree of safety before it scrambles. It is no wonder that recipes tell you to cook custard gently using a double boiler.

Other Ingredients Influence Protein Coagulation

Other ingredients can greatly influence the temperature at which proteins cook.

Acids

Acidic ingredients can make proteins lose their charge so they no longer repel each other, and this can make proteins unwind (denature). Custards with acidic ingredients like fruits or vegetables will cook sooner than those without.

Acids can completely "cook" proteins with no heat at all. Lime juice cooks scallops in ceviche. This is not to say it will be safe to eat as raw fish contains many other things that will not be killed by the acid. Some marinated shrimp recipes contain too much vinegar and produce tough "overcooked" shrimp.

Sugar

Large molecules, like sugar, probably delay protein coagulation simply by being in the way and slowing down the joining of unwound proteins as they bump into each other. A custard with extra sugar will take longer to cook. Of course, the amount of proteins you have will influence how quickly a custard will set, too. If you add an extra whole egg or yolks or whites, the custard will set sooner.

Starches

Starch granules swell with heat and can be very large. The exact nature of the way starches prevent protein coagulation is not known. It may be as simple as the swollen starch granules physically keeping the denatured proteins apart. Most household starches (cornstarch, flour, arrowroot powder) prevent eggs from coagulating in a custard or dairy proteins from forming curds in sauces.

STUCK! WHY DO PROTEINS STICK?

Once upon a time, a long time ago in the 1950s (before the days of nonstick cookware), my former husband and I started a boys boarding school, Brandon Hall. Thank goodness we started with just a few boys. I knew very little about cooking, and scrambling eggs was the bane of my existence. I would frantically stir, trying to keep the eggs from sticking to the pan. They stuck all the more. I scrambled a dozen eggs at a time, but with my frantic stirring, they just came out a small, knotty mess.

Fortunately, my German mother-in-law, Anna Hecht, came to visit and showed me how to scramble eggs. Heat the empty pan first! She got the pan hot, then poured in a little oil and tilted the pan to coat. Next, she poured in the beaten eggs and simply allowed them to stand on the heat for what seemed like forever. If she thought that they were cooking too fast, she lifted the pan from the heat, but did not stir. When the eggs began to set, she took a big spatula and pushed the curds to one side, which allowed the uncooked eggs to come in contact with the pan. With just a few strokes of the spatula, she could make two eggs puff and look like more than my dozen.

Heat the Empty Skillet First

Heating the empty skillet is the big secret. The metal expands, closing some imperfections and creating a hot surface. Eggs are liquid protein. When I poured them into the cold skillet, they ran into every pit and scratch in the metal. Then when I heated the pan, I was literally cooking the eggs into the pan. With the pan hot first, the eggs cooked on the surface, not down in it.

Grandmama Hecht waited until the eggs were set before she shoved them to the side. A major part of sticking is whether the food in the pan is done. When foods cook, the proteins coagulate, and the granules absorb water, swell, pop, and exude starch, which thickens any free liquid—the food becomes firmer. When this firmer state is reached, food usually stops sticking.

With many foods, the hotter, now dry, food surface browns. When this surface browning occurs, the food is no longer stuck to the pan. This happens with foods sautéed on the stovetop as well as with baked goods in the oven.

Let's follow the preparation of boneless chicken fillets—a quick, delicious dish with a fabulous reduction sauce. For two breasts, use a 10-inch skillet (not a nonstick skillet—you get better browning with a regular heavy skillet). HEAT THE EMPTY SKILLET FIRST! It should not be smoking hot, but hot enough that the upper edge of the pan is hot to a quick touch. Lift the skillet off the heat; pour in two tablespoons of vegetable oil and tilt the pan to run the oil over its surface. Place the pan back on the heat and immediately add the chicken breasts, rib-side up. The breasts sizzle and stick to the hot pan. You can see that they are really STUCK! Don't panic and start chiseling at them. They are not going to come loose.

Leave It Alone until It Browns

As Chris Tracy at Calphalon says, "This is a Zen moment!" Think happy thoughts. All is right with the world. Look to the heavens. Have a sip of zinfandel, if you are desperate—just don't touch the chicken!

After about ninety seconds, which seems like an eternity, the breasts brown and release from the pan all by themselves. You simply slip a spatula under each and flip them over. Now they are stuck on the other side—another Zen moment. You have to leave them alone until they brown. Then they are free, unstuck, and you can transfer them to a serving platter.

Add half a cup of liquid—chicken stock or white wine

works best—to the pan. Scrape up any browned stuck-on particles from the pan, add herbs, and reduce the liquid over high heat until only a few tablespoons remain. Stir in a little heavy cream and cook until the sauce thickens. Spoon this sauce over the chicken, garnish, and serve. (See the exact recipe below.)

The same technique applies to cooking other meats with a quick reduction sauce. You could use a fish fillet, pork, lamb, or beef (see the following recipe, Salmon Fillets with Sweet Mustard Dill Glaze)—whatever the meat, when you drop it into the hot pan, it gets stuck and stays stuck until it browns and releases all by itself.

All these same steps occur in the oven. If you grease or spray a pan with nonstick cooking spray (which you could also have used in the skillet on the stovetop) and bake a cake, muffins, or cookies until the bottoms are lightly browned, they will release from and come out of the pan nicely.

Overview: To minimize sticking, grease (use oil, melted shortening, or butter with oil) or spray a pan with nonstick cooking spray and be patient! Wait until the food is done or lightly browned to remove it. The recipes that follow illustrate easy stovetop nonstick cooking.

LEMON CHICKEN WITH THYME

A quick, delicious dish: seared boneless chicken breasts with a classic reduction sauce. Dinner for two, ready in minutes. I love to serve this with fresh asparagus that has been tossed with oil and cooked under the broiler for four minutes and/or tomato halves with a spoon of vinaigrette on each, topped with buttered breadcrumbs and broiled until the breadcrumbs are browned.

What This Recipe Shows

Preheating an empty pan prevents sticking.

Waiting until the chicken browns allows it to release itself from the pan.

Alcohol dissolves and frees water-soluble, fat-soluble, and other flavors that are neither water- nor fat-soluble.

Tips for making a successful reduction sauce: good wine, low-sodium stock, cook off all the wine before adding the cream, don't over reduce the cream sauce (see the section "Reduction Sauces: Tips for Successful Reduction Sauces" in Chapter Five: Perfect Sauces for the reasons).

---

2 medium boneless, skinless chicken breasts
Finely ground sea salt and ground pepper
½ cup buttermilk
½ teaspoon fine sea salt
2 tablespoons very mild olive oil or vegetable oil
½ cup dry white wine like sauvignon blanc
¼ cup low-sodium chicken stock
½ teaspoon granular chicken bouillon
1 teaspoon fresh thyme leaves
1 bay leaf
⅓ cup heavy cream
Zest of 1 lemon

Sprinkle the chicken breasts with the salt and pepper. Place each breast between multiple pieces of wax paper and pound from the middle to the edges to make the breast more equal in thickness, about ¼ inch thick. Place the buttermilk in a heavy-duty zip-top plastic freezer bag and add the salt. Add the chicken breasts to the buttermilk mixture and seal the bag. Refrigerate for an hour or two. Remove the chicken from the bag, pat dry, and let warm up for 15 to 30 minutes or so before cooking.

Heat a 10-inch skillet over medium to medium-high heat until the upper edge of the pan feels hot to a quick touch or a drop of water sizzles lightly in the pan. Remove from the heat; pour in the oil and tilt the pan to run the oil over its surface. Return the pan to the heat and immediately place the breasts in the pan with the rib side up. The breasts will sizzle and stick to the pan. After at least 90 seconds, the breasts will brown and release from the pan all by themselves. If they are browning too quickly, lift them off the heat briefly. Turn each over. Again, they will stick. Wait until they brown on the second side and release and are thoroughly cooked, then transfer them to a covered platter. You may need to adjust the heat to low and cover the pan to cook a bit more, or finish the cooking in the oven.

Pour the wine and stock into the hot pan. Scrape the pan to loosen any stuck-on particles. Add the bouillon, thyme, and bay leaf. Bring to a boil over high heat and cook until only a few tablespoons of liquid remain. Stir in the cream and cook until the sauce thickens, then stir in the lemon zest. Remove the bay leaf. Spoon the boiling sauce over the chicken and serve immediately. For another delicious reduction sauce for chicken see the Apple Orange Sauce, below.

Makes 2 servings

APPLE ORANGE SAUCE

A slightly sweet sauce for chicken or pork with apple and a hint of orange—delicious!

What This Recipe Shows

Intensely flavored orange zest adds zip and flavor.

½ cup apple juice
½ teaspoon ground sage
¼ cup apple jelly or apricot preserves
2 tablespoons amaretto liqueur
Zest of 1 orange

After cooking the chicken breasts as in the Lemon Thyme Chicken recipe, make the following reduction sauce in the skillet rather than the lemon thyme sauce. Add the apple juice to the hot skillet. Scrape the pan to remove any stuck-on particles. Add the sage and apple jelly or apricot preserves. Boil until reduced by half. Add the amaretto and cook for 1 minute. Add the orange zest. Return the mixture to a boil and cook until reduced to a sauce. Pour the sauce over the chicken and serve hot.

Makes 4 servings

SALMON FILLETS
WITH SWEET MUSTARD DILL GLAZE

The hint of sweet apple gives an interesting complexity to the mustard and perfectly sets off the salmon.

1 medium (12-ounce) skinless salmon fillet
¼ teaspoon finely ground sea salt
⅛ teaspoon ground pepper
2 tablespoons very mild olive oil
3 tablespoons water
4 tablespoons apple jelly
⅓ cup coarse mustard
1 teaspoon chopped fresh dill, plus several sprigs for
  garnish

Sprinkle the salmon with the salt and pepper on each side and rub them over the fish.

Heat a 10-inch skillet over medium to medium-high heat until the upper edge of the pan feels hot to a quick touch. Remove the pan from the heat; pour in the oil and tilt the pan to run the oil over the surface of the pan. Return the pan to the heat and immediately place the salmon in the pan. The salmon will sizzle and stick to the pan. After at least 90 seconds, the salmon will brown and release from the pan all by itself. Slip a spatula under it and turn it over. Again, it will stick. Wait again until it is brown on the second side and releases. You will be able to see from the side how deeply the fillet is cooked. Cover the pan, lower the heat if needed, and cook the salmon for a few minutes more until cooked thoroughly, then transfer it to a platter.

Add the water, apple jelly, and mustard to the hot pan. Scrape the pan to loosen any stuck-on particles. Bring to a boil and cook, stirring continuously, until the sauce thickens and only a few tablespoons of liquid remain.

Remove from the heat. Stir in the chopped dill and spread the sauce over the salmon. Garnish with sprigs of dill.

Makes 4 servings

BRINING

Brining is an effective way to increase the juiciness of cooked muscle fibers (meat, fish, or fowl). Dr. Estes Reynolds, meat expert at the University of Georgia, explains that liquid loss in normal cooking can be as high as 30 percent. But, if you brine the meat, fish, or fowl before cooking, the liquid loss can be as low as 15 percent. This can mean a wonderfully juicy turkey!

How Brining Works

Brining works in a number of ways to increase juiciness. Dr. Reynolds explains that salt causes some of the proteins in muscle fibers to denature (unwind and swell), exposing bonding sites. Water can bind directly to some of these sites. More important, with more bonding sites exposed, liquid is trapped when the meat cooks and the proteins bind together. As long as you do not overcook the meat, a lot of the natural juices will be retained.

Not only are more natural juices bound and held during cooking, but meats also absorb liquid during brining. Some of this is by osmosis—liquid going through cell walls into the cells. We can verify that brined meat absorbs liquid if we weigh a product before and after brining and noting the weight increase. Dr. Reynolds estimates that this water uptake is between 6 and 8 percent.

Another way in which brining increases juiciness is that some of the proteins in muscle fiber dissolve in salt water, so that proteins that were solid become liquid.

Of all the things going on, the major juiciness enhancer is salt, which is causing the denaturation and accompanying expansion or swelling of the proteins and exposure of many bonding sites.

To Brine or Not to Brine

Whenever you want to make meat moister or juicier, think about brining. Shrimp are wonderful brined—so are fish fillets, chicken pieces, and whole chickens. I also brine pork, which is now bred so lean that it easily dries out during cooking. Brining can improve pork considerably. High-fat cuts like a pork butt are juicy without brining. I would not brine a steak. Steaks are tender cuts of meat, and are best cooked fast using a high-heat method like grilling or broiling. With fast, high-heat cooking, as long as you do not overcook the meat, moisture is retained. A well-marbled steak cooked medium-rare can be very juicy.

How to Brine

The amount of salt and the length of time that you brine depends on the size and shape of the cut or piece of meat. A large turkey (eighteen pounds or so) should be brined slowly overnight. Dr. Reynolds suggests a brine of 9.6 ounces of salt per gallon of liquid. One cup of table salt weighs 10.2 ounces, so a scant cup of table salt per gallon of liquid is close enough.

If you are using kosher salt, which dissolves nine times faster (for Diamond Crystal kosher), the amounts will be different. Diamond Crystal kosher salt weighs only 5 ounces per cup, so you will need 2 cups per gallon for the brine. Morton kosher salt weighs 7-plus ounces, so you will need 1⅓ to 1½ cups per gallon for the brine.

Any nonreactive container is fine to use for brining. Since it is hard to find something big enough to soak a turkey in, I use a turkey cooking bag. I put the turkey in the bag and then place it in a large bowl to securely hold it. You need to completely cover the bird with liquid. As you add water to the bag, measure how much it takes. If it takes a gallon, add 1 cup of salt. If it takes 1½ gallons, go with a light 1½ cups. The turkey must be refrigerated during brining. There will be increased bacteria growth if the turkey is not refrigerated.

You can rub the salt directly onto the turkey first, before submerging it in water, or, for a flavor rub, you can use herbs and salt. Mix your choice of dried herbs (thyme, oregano, parsley, whatever) and salt and rub the inside and outside of the turkey well. If you use a little less salt than you think your amount of liquid will indicate, you can add more salt after you have added the liquid.

You can use liquids other than water to make your brine. Apple juice is a popular liquid for brining a chicken or turkey.

I asked Dr. Reynolds about using sugar. He said that the only reason for sugar in a brine would be for flavor. Sugar has no technical function; salt is the key ingredient.

Size and Shape Should Determine How You Brine

With small pieces like shrimp or thin fish fillets, you can brine effectively in a very short time with a concentrated brine. For 1½ pounds of extra-large shrimp in their shells, I put them in a nonreactive container, sprinkle ¼ cup table salt (use less salt if using peeled shrimp) on them, barely cover them with ice water (about 1 quart), and allow them to stand for about 30 minutes. For thin fish fillets, I may use ¼ cup table salt and less than a quart of water, but allow them to stand for just 10 minutes. For a large roasting hen (5 to 6 pounds), I would use ½ cup salt in a little over a quart of water and let it stand for 3 to 4 hours.

With all brining, it is vital that you rinse the surface salt off well before cooking. A properly brined product should never taste salty. It should be juicy, with good flavor. If you brine with too much salt for too long, the food will not only be salty, it can also be dry.

In summary, brining can give you wonderfully enhanced, juicy, flavorful poultry, seafood, or even pork. Remember, always refrigerate during brining, rinse well after brining, and do not overcook!

Brining Times for a Basic Brine	
Whole chicken	4 hours
Chicken pieces	2 hours with a basic brine or 1 hour with a more concentrated brine
Cornish hens	1 hour
Turkey breast	4 to 6 hours
Pork chops	4 hours

BRINED SHRIMP IN GARLIC BUTTER

This recipe was inspired by Giuliano Hazan's Shrimp in Garlic Butter. I have brined the shrimp and slightly altered the ingredients. Absolutely luscious!

What This Recipe Shows

Brining produces incredibly juicy proteins.

1½ pounds extra-large shrimp, peeled and deveined
2 tablespoons sea salt per quart of water
½ cup (1 stick) butter
½ cup olive oil
3 large shallots, minced very finely
5 garlic cloves, smashed and minced
Zest and juice of 1 lemon
4 green onions, white and some green parts, sliced into
    thin rounds

Place the shrimp in a large nonreactive bowl. Add the salt and enough cold water just to cover. Refrigerate for 30 minutes. Drain and rinse well: repeat several times. Spread the shrimp out on paper towels to dry.

Preheat the broiler. In a medium saucepan, melt the butter over medium heat. Add the oil, shallots, garlic, and lemon zest and juice. Reduce the heat to low.

Spread the shrimp out in a single layer in a large ovenproof glass baking dish. Pour the butter mixture over the shrimp and broil for about 7 minutes. Turn the shrimp over and broil for about 7 minutes until the shrimp turn pink and are thoroughly cooked. Remove the shrimp and transfer to a serving platter. Serve sprinkled with the green onions.

For a lighter version, brine the shrimp as above in 3 tablespoons of salt per 3 quarts of water, rinse very well and dry. Toss the shrimp in 2 tablespoons of high-smoke-point olive oil. Lay shrimp tightly packed on a broiler pan. Broil for 5 to 7 minutes per side until done. Heat 2 tablespoons of olive oil in a pan over medium heat, tilting a little to pool the oil if needed. Add shallots and garlic and cook for a few minutes, being careful not to burn the garlic (it can burn easily, turning bitter and brown). Add lemon zest, scallions, and shrimp, stirring to coat all well. Add 1 tablespoon of butter and, optionally, lemon juice and stir and serve.

Makes 4 servings

BROWNING

Have you ever had a dish that was deep brown on the outside but almost raw in the middle? This can happen with fairly thin pieces of food that do not take long to cook through. Why did it brown so fast? Or you may have had a delicious dish, but it was disgustingly pale and unappetizing looking. What can you do to make it a deeper, richer brown?

The Big Factors in Browning: Proteins, Reducing Sugars, and Reduced Acidity

Protein, certain sugars, and acidity are the big three in browning. The more protein and reducing sugars (like glucose in corn syrup) a dish has, and the less acidity (more alkalinity), the browner the dish will be. Some examples are:

- Glazes for roasting: Glazes that contain protein or sugar will brown faster. A chicken brushed with melted butter (which contains both protein and sugar) will brown faster than one brushed with oil. A mixture of melted butter and dark corn syrup or brown sugar will give you a rich, dark glaze.
- Sugar in a breading or coating may cause the food to brown too fast.
- To make any baked goods (cookies, cakes, muffins) browner, increase the protein in the batter (not just the glaze) by adding egg yolk or whole egg; switch to a higher protein flour like unbleached or bread flour; and/or increase the sugar. Lowering the acidity (cutting out any acidic ingredient) or adding a tiny amount of baking soda (not too much or you risk preventing proper leavening) can make baked goods browner, too.

Whenever you need to make something browner or less brown, think of creative ways to alter the big three—protein, sugar, or acidity—to get your dish exactly the color you want. The following recipe illustrates this with proteins in the butter and sugars in the corn syrup for browning.

FAMOUS CRAB CAKES

This recipe is my modification of Chef Kevin Walker's Famous Crab Cakes. They are magnificent golden brown cakes—chunks of crabmeat bound together by delicious, flavorful mayonnaise with just a bare minimum of cracker crumbs to hold moisture.

What This Recipe Shows

The egg already in the mayonnaise, with the addition of a little extra egg, holds the crab pieces together.

Brushing with melted butter, which provides protein, and a small amount of corn syrup (a sugar) produces excellent browning.

¾ cup Crab Mayonnaise for East Coast Crab (recipe follows)

1¼ pounds fresh crabmeat, carefully picked over to remove any shell

2 ounces saltine crackers (about 6), crushed well into crumbs

6 tablespoons butter, melted

1 teaspoon light corn syrup

Preheat the oven to 375°F and arrange an oven rack slightly above the center of the oven.

In a large bowl, combine the mayonnaise, crabmeat, and cracker crumbs. Shape the mixture into 6 cakes and place the cakes on a baking sheet.

In a small bowl, stir together the melted butter and corn syrup and brush the cakes with this mixture. Bake for 20 to 25 minutes, until browned, firm, and cooked thoroughly.

Makes 3 servings

Crab Mayonnaise for East Coast Crab

⅛ cup mayonnaise
0.6 large egg (beat an egg and use slightly more than half)
1 scant teaspoon Old Bay seasoning (see Note)
1 scant teaspoon Dijon mustard
1 teaspoon sugar
½ teaspoon dry mustard
¼ teaspoon finely ground sea salt
1 tablespoon dry white wine
⅓ teaspoon Worcestershire sauce
Zest of ¼ lemon

In a small bowl, stir together the mayonnaise, egg, Old Bay, Dijon, sugar, dry mustard, salt, wine, Worcestershire sauce, and lemon zest. Use this mayonnaise in cooked recipes only, as shown here, since it contains raw egg.

Makes about ¾ cup

NOTE: For delicate West Coast Dungeness crab, omit the Old Bay seasoning.

Nonenzymatic Browning at a Glance	
What to Do for More Browning	**Why**
Increase the amount of sugar or protein in batters or glazes.	Sugar and proteins are necessary for browning at lower temperatures.
Substitute corn syrup for all or part of the sugar.	Glucose browns at lower temperatures than other sugars.
What to Do for More Browning	**Why**
Add baking soda.	Reducing acidity enhances browning.
What to Do for Less Browning	
Reduce the amount of or remove sugars.	
Reduce the amount of or remove proteins.	
Add acidic ingredients like lemon juice.	

MORE ABOUT THE MAILLARD REACTION

As I said in chapter one on flavor, the Maillard reaction is a series of complex reactions between sugars and proteins that produce caramelized browning at lower temperatures, giving foods a rich-tasting brown coating.

Sugar's contribution to browning has far-reaching effects. For instance, when potatoes are refrigerated for several days, the low temperature causes some of their starch to break down into sugars. These potatoes will brown much faster than potatoes that were not refrigerated. Early in the season, when the starch content of potatoes is very high, starch on the surface of french fries can limit browning, since the sugars, which brown faster, are covered by starch. Rinsing the potatoes several times in water can eliminate this problem.

If you baste your meat with something that contains sugar and protein, it will get much browner than if you baste with oil. My favorite basting combination is a little corn syrup (for the fast-browning glucose), butter (which contains both sugar and protein from milk), and consommé (clarified beef stock and gelatin, both of which contain proteins to aid browning).

Tough or Tender

Some muscles are tender and some are tough. Frequently used muscles will be tough but flavorful; they can be moist-cooked (slow cooked) to dissolve tough connective tissue and served with gravy or in cooking liquid to make up for lack of juiciness. The recipe that follows is an incredibly delicious example of this. The sauce is amazingly wonderful.

FALL-APART-TENDER SLOW ROAST PORK

This is lean meat in an incredibly delicious sauce. It is an ideal dish to prepare ahead for a crowd or big family dinner—very easy, with hearty, marvelous flavors. During the slow cooking, flavorful tissues in the meat will break down into liquid and are now in the sauce. So it is vital to serve the meat in this flavorful sauce.

What This Recipe Shows

Cooking meat slowly in a generous amount of braising liquid at a lower temperature produces a wonderfully tender dish.

Pork butt, a less expensive cut that is frequently avoided because of its fat and connective tissue, is ideal for slow cooking, which dissolves both fat and connective tissue.

---

1 bone-in pork shoulder roast (Boston butt roast)
    (4 to 6 pounds), trimmed of fat
¾ to 1 cup Worcestershire sauce
1 to 1⅓ cup light brown sugar
3 cups unsweetened apple juice
½ teaspoon salt
2 tablespoons cornstarch
¼ cup cold water

Arrange a shelf slightly below the center of the oven and preheat the oven to 350°F.

Place the pork in a nonreactive pot or casserole with a tight-fitting lid that is just large enough to hold it. Boil the apple juice for 5 minutes and pour it carefully over the pork. The juice should cover at least half of the roast. Sprinkle the pork with the Worcestershire sauce, then press the brown sugar over the pork to form a crust. Cover tightly with the lid. Place in the oven and bake for 4 to 5 hours, turning the roast over every hour, until the meat is so tender that it pulls apart easily. If the meat does not pull apart easily, return the casserole to the oven and bake, covered, for 30 minutes more. Check again and bake 30 minutes more as needed. Remove the meat from the sauce and transfer to a bowl. Pull the meat apart into big chunks and remove the bone. Pour the sauce into a gravy separator or Pyrex bowl. Skim the fat off the top and return sauce to the pan. Stir the salt into the sauce. (*Do not omit the salt.* It is vital for the taste of the dish.) In a small bowl, stir together the cornstarch and water. Stir the cornstarch mixture into the sauce. Place the casserole on medium heat and cook, stirring, until the sauce thickens.

Serve the meat in its delicious sauce, hot or at room temperature.

Makes about 6 servings

NOTE: This can easily be done in a slow cooker. Cover and cook on high for 6 to 7 hours or until the meat pulls apart easily.

More Tips for Tender Meat

Muscles that are not used as much, like those in the center of the back—the loin—are naturally tender. Well-marbled meat will be juicier and more tender. And slicing meat into very thin slices across the grain produces "tender," easily chewable pieces, even from a tough cut. The two recipes that follow illustrate how important it is to notice the direction of the grain. In skirt steak, the grain runs from side to side, so it is vital to slice the steak lengthwise. In flank steak, the grain runs up and down, so it must be sliced crosswise.

FLAVORFUL SKIRT STEAK

Browned, crusty steak sliced very thin (lengthwise)—incredibly delicious.

What This Recipe Shows

Salt in the soy sauce and the seasoning brine the meat for juiciness.

Slicing the meat across (perpendicular to) the grain makes this tough cut easily chewable.

½ cup mild olive oil or vegetable oil
¼ cup soy sauce
2 teaspoons McCormick's Montreal steak seasoning
1 tablespoon dark brown sugar
1 pound skirt steak, cut into about 5-inch pieces

In a heavy-duty plastic freezer bag, combine the oil, soy sauce, steak seasoning, and brown sugar. Add the steak, seal the bag, and marinate in the refrigerator overnight or for at least several hours. Turn the bag over halfway through the marinating as the marinade tends to separate. Pat the steak dry and oil the steak lightly on both sides.

Heat a cast-iron skillet over medium heat. Place the skirt steak in the skillet and slightly press down on it to create a sear. Cook for 3 or 4 minutes, then flip the steak and cook for an additional 3 or 4 minutes or until desired doneness. Remove the steak from the heat and allow to stand covered for 10 minutes.

Notice that the grain of the meat runs side to side. It is vital to slice across (perpendicular to) the grain to tenderize. This means you will slice the steak lengthwise into very thin slices. Slicing very thin across the grain improves tenderness. This is a tough cut of meat. To further improve tenderness, remove any membrane and also pound very well to tenderize any tough connective tissue before marinating and cooking. Marinate the pounded steak for a shorter time than an unpounded steak. Pour any drippings over the slices of steak and serve.

Makes 2 servings

FLAVORFUL FLANK STEAK (LONDON BROIL)

A browned, crusty, tender steak sliced thin (crosswise)—also incredibly delicious!

½ cup mild olive oil or vegetable oil with a high smoke point
¼ cup soy sauce
2 teaspoons McCormick's Montreal steak seasoning
2 tablespoons dark brown sugar
2 pounds flank steak (London broil), slightly kidney shaped for the tenderest cut

In a heavy-duty plastic freezer bag, combine the oil, soy sauce, steak seasoning, and brown sugar. Add the steak, seal the bag, and marinate in the refrigerator overnight or for at least several hours. Turn the bag over halfway through the marinating as the marinade tends to separate.

Preheat the broiler to high. Oil the steak lightly on both sides with a high-smoke-point oil. Place the steak on a broiler pan and place the pan about 4 inches from the broiler. Broil the steak for about 8 minutes, then flip and broil for an additional 10 minutes or so.

A steak about ¾ inch thick on one end and ½ inch on the other end was tender and thoroughly cooked using the 8- and 10-minute cooking times and was very tender when sliced across the grain. Add additional cooking time for thicker steaks. Remove the steak from the broiler and let stand tented with foil on the broiler pan for 10 minutes.

Notice that the grain of the meat runs lengthwise. It is vital to slice across (perpendicular to) the grain to tenderize. This means you will slice the steak crosswise into thin slices. Pour any drippings over the slices of steak and serve.

Makes 4 servings

TENDERIZERS

In an effort to tenderize, marinades may contain ingredients with enzymes that break down meat fibers like pineapple, papaya, kiwi, ginger, figs, or honeydew, or they may contain acids like citrus juice or vinegar to denature proteins. Unfortunately, the enzymes turn the surface of the meat to mush, while the interior remains untouched and tough. And poking holes in the meat to get the enzymes into the interior will cause greater loss of juices.

My experience with tenderizing enzymes can be summarized by the title of a book edited by the famous Oxford physicist Dr. Nicholas Kurti and his wife, Giana: *But the Crackling Is Superb*. This was the result of a grand scheme they had to tenderize a roast with pineapple juice. The roast was an inedible mush, but they did manage to fry the skin into crisp strips, thus the title.

MARINADES

Technically, marinades are supposed to tenderize and add flavor. Marinades are very successful at adding flavor, but, with the exception of dairy products, they are a disaster at tenderizing. Dairy products are, in my opinion, the only marinades that truly tenderize. Hunters have long been known to marinate tough game in milk. Indian recipes use yogurt marinades. Southern cooks soak their chicken in buttermilk before frying. Harold McGee points out that the calcium in these dairy products activates enzymes in the meat to tenderize in much the same way that aging does. But with nondairy marinades, the meat is toughened because the marinade is too acidic, and/or the meat is left in the marinade too long.

Think of all the tough marinated shrimp you've had. They are tough because they were left too long in a marinade that was too acidic, and they are just as "overcooked" as they would be if they had been boiled for an hour.

It is possible to make a marinade that does not toughen shrimp. For my delicious marinated shrimp in *CookWise*, I layered the shrimp with thin slices of onions and used only 2 tablespoons vinegar and 2 tablespoons caper juice to 1 cup oil.

Cuts of meat, like flank steak, that are not as delicate as shrimp survive marinating better. Fortunately, most marinades penetrate foods by only a fraction of an inch. So even those containing ½ cup citrus juice and/or vinegar or wine do not toughen flank steak too much. Marinades also impart excellent flavor. If a flank steak, especially a steak with a slight kidney shape, is cooked medium-rare or even medium or medium-well and sliced thinly across the grain, it will be tender. But this is due to proper selection, cooking, and slicing, not the marinade.

Here is an example of a marinade used for flavor.

MARINATED ONIONS

A true classic party recipe—guests hover over the bowl and ask, "What is this wonderful dip?" It's so easy that I am almost embarrassed to tell them. Many years ago, Martha Summerhour, a genteel Southern lady, shared this recipe with me, and I thank her, party after party.

What This Recipe Shows

Vinegar and sugar smooth out the sharpness in onions or even hot chiles.

Squeezing moisture from the onions prevents the dip from becoming watery.

---

3 large sweet onions (Vidalia, Walla Walla, or Texas)
½ cup apple cider vinegar
1 cup sugar
2 cups water
1 cup good-quality mayonnaise
1 teaspoon celery salt
½ teaspoon finely ground sea salt
2 packages (around 8 ounces) sea salt bagel chips or
 other salty snack crackers

Chop the onions to a medium-fine dice in a food processor or by hand.

In a medium bowl, stir together the vinegar, sugar, and water. Add the onions and marinate in the refrigerator for at least several hours or up to overnight.

Drain the onions, then place them on a clean, smooth-textured towel and gently squeeze them to remove more liquid.

In a medium bowl, stir together well the onions, mayonnaise, celery salt, and sea salt. Serve cold, with the bagel chips or salty crackers.

Makes 8 servings as an hors d'oeuvre

OVEN-ROASTED
HERBED CHICKEN BREAST

Flavorful, crunchy-crusted, moist, tender chicken breast. Incredibly delicious!

What This Recipe Shows

Since boneless, skinless chicken breasts are small, even a weak brine for a short time adds a little moisture.

Buttermilk contains calcium and acts as a tenderizer.

4 small boneless, skinless chicken breasts
½ cup buttermilk
½ teaspoon fine sea salt
Dash of hot sauce
2 tablespoons light brown sugar
Nonstick spray
1½ cups Pepperidge Farm Herbed-Seasoned Stuffing
½ cup freshly grated Parmesan cheese
4 tablespoons (½ stick) butter, melted

Place a chicken breast on the counter between two pieces of waxed paper. Hit the thicker end with a meat pounder to flatten it so the breast is an even thickness all over, about a quarter of an inch thick. Repeat with each breast.

In a heavy-duty zip-top plastic freezer bag, add the buttermilk, salt, hot sauce, and brown sugar. Add the chicken breasts to the buttermilk mixture and seal the bag. Refrigerate for an hour or two.

Arrange a shelf in the center of the oven and preheat the oven to 375°F. Spray a heavy baking sheet with nonstick spray.

In a food processor or blender, combine the stuffing and Parmesan and process into medium-fine crumbs. Stir in the butter. Spread the crumb mixture over a plate.

Drain the chicken breasts and discard the marinade. Press each breast thoroughly into the crumb mixture to coat both sides.

Arrange the chicken breasts on the prepared baking sheet. Sprinkle any remaining crumbs on top of the chicken breasts.

Roast for about 20 minutes, until the coating is crisp and the chicken is cooked through. For a lighter version, half the cheese and butter, and bake on a broiler pan to allow the underside to crisp.

Makes 4 servings

MOPS AND SOPS

Mops and sops are sauces that are normally applied during the last hour of cooking. Tomato- or ketchup-based barbecue-type sauces that contain some kind of sugar (molasses or brown sugar) to aid in browning are the most commonly used, though there are thousands of gourmet grilling sauces, white barbecue sauces, etc.

RUBS

Flavor-packed rubs can be dry or wet mixtures of spices and herbs that are rubbed directly onto the food before cooking.

BRINES

As discussed earlier in the section on brining, brining adds liquid to cells and makes meat juicier. Liquid flows through cell walls toward the most concentrated side. You would think that heavily salted water would draw water out of meat cells, but the interior of the meat cells is more concentrated than the heavily salted water, so liquid does go into the meat cells. Meat increases in weight during brining, and once you have experienced how juicy a brined roast chicken or turkey is, you can never do it any other way.

So, which should you use: a brine, marinade, rub, or sauce? I have read recipes from barbecue champions who used all four in one dish. They brined the chicken for two to three hours, then marinated it, then used a rub, and finally finished it off with a sauce. Whatever works for you, go with it.

AGING AND TENDERNESS

I was once on a panel with a noted seafood expert and chef when someone asked how he selected his fish. He said that he, personally, went every morning to the dock and selected fish for the restaurant for the day. I expected him to emphasize things like "firm flesh, shiny and transparent eyes, dark pink to bright red gills," but this was not what he said at all. He said that he would not buy a fish unless it was "stiff as a board" (in rigor). I had never thought about fish going through rigor.

All animal muscles have their own storage supply of glycogen or carbohydrates, which they burn for energy. This process creates lactic acid as a waste product. When circulation stops, blood no longer flows through the muscles and this lactic acid is not removed. In addition to the protein myosin, muscles contain another protein called actin, which normally slides past the myosin during muscle movement. When lactic acid builds up in the muscles, the actin and myosin that normally slide past each other react chemically to form actomyosin. This causes muscles to contract tightly and become, as the seafood expert said, stiff as a board.

Eventually, though, the muscles relax again. The internal temperature and the species are the two major determinants of how long it takes muscles to go into rigor and how long they stay in that state. Rigor takes about a day to pass in beef, for example, but only about six hours in pork and chicken.

Going through rigor improves meat in several ways. First, it greatly improves the meat's texture; meat that does not go through rigor has a gummy texture. Second, the increase in acidity slows the spoilage of the meat and also enhances the water-holding ability of the meat proteins. Meat that has been allowed to go through rigor properly is juicier than meat that has not.

It is very important that animals not be under stress or working hard just before slaughter. If they are, their muscles will have used up their supply of glycogen or carbohydrates and lactic acid will not have formed. The resulting meat will therefore be less acidic, darker in color, more easily spoiled, and will have a poorer texture.

Meat is hung at moderate temperatures (61°F) for sixteen to twenty hours postmortem to enhance its tenderness and ensure it proceeds into rigor. The hanging is done to stretch out the muscles before rigor sets in. If the muscles are allowed to contract as rigor starts, the bonding of the actin and myo-sin is stronger and the meat will be tougher. The reason for keeping the temperature moderate is that rapid chilling of meat before it goes into rigor will toughen it.

When we get a dark, poor-textured piece of meat at the market, or a piece that should be tender but is very tough, it may have been poorly processed. Even fish can be tough if not allowed to go through rigor properly.

Meat benefits greatly both in texture and flavor from aging after rigor. Aged meat has a buttery texture and a more intense meaty flavor. Meat should be held at 32°F to 36°F to control bacterial growth. An optimal aging period for beef is eleven days. Aging can be hastened by holding meat at a warmer temperature (70°F) for two days under high humidity (85 to 90 percent) to prevent moisture loss and with ultravio-let lights to control bacteria. The meat found in most markets is fast aged and gets a little additional aging during shipping and in the store.

Meat can be aged wet (in vacuum-sealed packaging) or dry (exposed to the air). Nearly all meat today is wet aged. Because of the moisture and weight loss of costly meat, dry-aged prime beef is extremely expensive. Even if you are will-ing to pay the price, it is difficult to find—obtainable only from a handful of specialty suppliers.

FISH

Beef, pork, lamb, and fowl—familiar meats to cooks—are from warm-blooded animals. Fish, on the other hand, change body temperature with the temperature of the water. Land ani-mals' muscles must constantly fight gravity. Fish can remain effortlessly suspended in water, but when a fish moves, it must move against water, which requires much more force to push through than air. It is no surprise that fish muscles are completely different from those of land animals. And it should be no surprise that fish require different handling, storing, and cooking than other meats.

Handling Fish

Fish is highly perishable. The flesh of freshly caught fish is sterile, and bacterial spoilage does not begin until the fish has gone through and passed out of rigor. Rigor takes place sooner and lasts for a shorter period in fish than in mammals. The onset and duration of rigor can be prolonged by minimizing the struggle that the fish goes through and prompt chilling once the fish is caught. This can significantly prolong the period of freshness. Some fish, like halibut, have a long rigor and store better than most. In an ideal world, fish would be killed, gutted, and iced immediately. Then they would go into rigor and remain in rigor during the shipping period, arriving at our markets still in or just coming out of rigor—at the absolute peak of freshness. Also, if fish are gutted immediately, most parasites, which are in the gut, will be removed before they can move to the flesh.

Unfortunately, once the fish is out of rigor, marine microorganisms in the gills and the intestinal tract begin causing spoilage. Some of these microorganisms can flourish at temperatures even as cold as 18°F—well below freezing! You can fast-freeze and thaw fish with minimal damage; however, it deteriorates during frozen storage. In raw fish, the texture loses its springiness, and cooked fish becomes dry and tasteless.

Ideally, you want to buy the freshest fish that you can and cook and eat it that day.

To keep fish even one day in the refrigerator, place fillets or a whole fish in a large strainer set over a bowl, then pile ice high on top of the fish and refrigerate. The ice will keep the fish close to 32°F, and as it melts, it continually rinses bacteria off the fish.

Freshness

How can you tell if a fish is fresh? Appearance and odor can help. Fresh fish may have a seaweed smell, but should never have a fishy or ammonia smell, which indicates protein deterioration. The skin should be shining and iridescent, with a clear coating. The flesh should be soft, but spring back when touched. The eyes should be clear and bright, with jet-black pupils, flush with the flesh or slightly protruding, but never sunken. The underside of the gills should be bright pink to red, not gray.

When buying fillets, go by the smell and the texture. The flesh should not be flaking or falling apart. It should be firm and bounce back when touched, not mushy.

It's in the Genes

To bring some order to the many species of fish, fin fish are grouped into lean fish (fat content under 5 percent) and fat fish (fat content 5 to 20 percent). Lean fish are essentially white-fleshed fish with a mild, nonfishy taste. They can have a delicate texture, like sole, flounder, orange roughy, farm-raised catfish, skate, and pollock, or a firmer texture that holds together better for grilling, like cod, halibut, haddock, grouper, tilefish, snapper, and tilapia.

Fatty or oily fish, like mackerel, bluefish, and salmon, normally have colored flesh and a definite fishy taste. Salmon's pink color is due to astaxanthin, a carotenoid compound, and you see some salmon that are deep in color and others that are pale. This depends on the availability of carotenoid compounds in the fish's diet. Some cooks recommend using a lot of wine or vinegar or a strong-flavored sauce to mask the strong taste of fatty or oily fish. I say you should not think that you can do something in cooking that will make oily fish taste like a mild, lean fish. Regardless of the sauce, mackerel is going to taste fishy and full-flavored even when it is very fresh.

FINE STRUCTURE OF FISH MUSCLE

Land animals contain significant amounts of "red meat"— steady working muscle cells like those in the legs and thighs containing red myoglobin, which receives and holds oxygen from the blood ready for use.

The main muscle of a fish is the great lateral muscle. It burns glycogen, a carbohydrate, in the cell fluids ready for instant use, speed, and power. The "dark meat" in fish—meat containing myoglobin—is in a small superficial muscle that fans out on each side of the lateral muscle. This dark area just under the skin contains a high proportion of fat, which is unsaturated. During storage, the fat in this dark meat is catalyzed by iron from the heme pigment and goes rancid. In a restaurant, when I get a piece of fish with the skin on, and observe the dark area next to the skin, I carefully eat around it.

Fish muscle fibers are made of actin, myosin, and tropomyosin, plus sarcoplasmic protein, all of which are found in warm-blooded animals. However, the muscle fibers of meat are thin and long—some can be up to a foot long. Fish muscle fibers are thick and no longer than about an inch. They are stacked on top of each other in parallel layers like cord wood, with very thin sheets of connective tissue at each end of the stack of short fibers. These sheets of connective tissue are not only very thin, they are more heat labile than the connective tissue of meat. It does not take much heat for this connective tissue to melt away to gelatin, leaving the short fish fibers falling apart, or "flaking." Fish can literally fall apart when you are cooking it.

COOKING FISH

Fish, be it fatty/oily or lean, is extremely easy to overcook and dry out. Its connective tissue melts easily and the fish flakes or falls apart. If you are cooking a whole fish, the thin part near the tail may be done cooking first and fall off. Some cooks protect this area by covering it with foil so that it cooks more slowly. Or you can wrap a whole fish in cheesecloth so that it can be moved without falling apart. An ideal situation is to cook the whole fish on a heatproof serving platter so that you do not have to transfer it to another dish.

Studies cooking 1-inch-thick salmon steaks to an internal temperature of 167°F at three different temperatures—350°F, 400°F, and 500°F—indicated that palatability of the cooked fish was not affected by oven temperature, and baking time at 500°F was half that of the lowest temperature.

Using the same temperature oven (400°F) to cook fish to

four different internal temperatures—158°F, 167°F, 176°F, and 185°F—indicated that salmon baked to the highest internal temperature was judged highest in flavor, but was lower in moisture than those cooked to 167°F and 176°F. The salmon steak cooked to 158°F was judged lowest in flavor and desirability. I think a lot of this is personal preference.

In evaluating samples done at different times, researchers found that the sample rushed from oven to table always won, indicating how important it is to serve fish promptly.

My personal preference (which somewhat agrees with the studies) is that simplest is best. I cooked salmon for my husband (15 to 20 minutes at 375°F), but I really like lean fish. I love to cook fillets (½ to ¾ inch thick), uncovered, on an ungreased baking sheet at 500°F for about 7 minutes, or until thoroughly cooked, then sauce the fillets with crushed macadamia nuts lightly browned in butter, as in the following recipe.

SIMPLEST FISH FILLETS

I learned to cook fish fillets this way in Key Largo, Florida.

4 fillets lean fish, less than ½ inch thick each (if you have cod or haddock that is thicker, simply slice it on an angle into thinner fillets or, for a fish like tilapia, with one thick side, slice a horizontal piece off the thick side so it is an even thickness, about ¼ inch)
½ teaspoon fine sea salt
Quick Macadamia Butter (recipe follows), for serving

Preheat the oven to 500°F.

Place the fillets (lightly oiled with high-smoke-point oil) on a rimmed baking sheet. Bake for about 7 minutes, or until thoroughly cooked. Transfer the fish to a serving platter and sprinkle with the salt. Sauce with the macadamia butter and serve.

Makes 4 servings

Quick Macadamia Butter

4 ounces roasted salted macadamia nuts
4 tablespoons (½ stick) butter

Pour the macadamia nuts into a heavy-duty plastic freezer bag and seal. Place it on the counter and hit the nuts with a meat pounder or the bottom of a saucepan just to partially break them up.

In a medium skillet, melt the butter over medium heat. Add the nuts. Cook, stirring, until the nuts are lightly browned. Be careful as browning of butter can happen very quickly, and the nuts should be removed from heat and the pan quickly at that point. Remove from the heat and serve immediately. For a lighter version, sauté the nuts in 1 tablespoon of olive oil until fragrant. Stir in 1 tablespoon of butter and serve.

MARINATING FISH

Fish is naturally tender because of its short muscle fibers. Marinades, then, are for flavor, not for tenderizing. As the proteins join together, the fish becomes solid white. This is a good indication of when the fish is done—when the flesh goes from glassy to solid white.

Fish that is delicate and easy to cook is an ideal candidate for cooking with mild acids and has been prepared in this way for many years. Traditionally, limes, the most acidic of the citrus fruits, have been used to make ceviche, a dish of fresh fish, lime juice, onions, peppers, tomatoes, etc. Great care must be taken to ensure the fish is free from parasites and bacteria as "cooking" with lime will kill only some toxins and not parasites and other bacteria.

For more on fish, you may want to get a good basic fish cookbook like Shirley King's *Fish: the Basics*. Her father was a fisherman and her book is excellent.

EGGS

SIMPLE EGG COOKERY

When you have to search through a cloudy mess of feathered egg whites to find what's left of your poached egg, or half of your scrambled eggs are irretrievably plastered to the bottom of the pan, egg cookery can seem anything but simple.

POACHING

Poke around at a raw egg out of its shell and you'll see that there are two parts to the white. Part of the white is thick and clings tightly to the yolk, and the other part is thin and runny. It's the thin part that causes the cloudy mess of egg whites when poaching. Fresh eggs have practically all thick white, so they will poach beautifully, without any mess floating around in the water.

How can you tell if an egg is fresh? As eggs age, carbon dioxide that was dissolved in the egg white seeps out through the pores in the shell, and oxygen and gases in the air seep in. The older the egg, the more air has seeped in, and the larger the air cell.

You can tell if an egg is fresh by placing it in a bowl of tap water. If the egg lies flat on the bottom, it has a small air cell and is quite fresh. If the egg stands up and bobs on the bottom, it has a larger air cell and is not as fresh.

In the grocery store, very fresh eggs in excellent condition are graded AA. Grade AA eggs are not available in every store and they may cost a little more, but if you are buying eggs to poach, they are worth it.

Getting the egg to set or cook quickly helps to make a handsome poached egg. Both acid and salt make eggs coagulate (cook) faster. Many directions for poaching say to add a little vinegar (about 2 teaspoons for an 8- to 10-inch skillet) to the poaching liquid. Salt is effective, too—about ¾ teaspoon for an 8- to 10-inch skillet. When hard cooking eggs, salt is a better choice because acids make a hard-cooked egg more difficult to peel. When poaching, you can use either or both.

It is easy to overcook poached eggs and end up with a leathery, unpleasant object. If you heat proteins gently, they unwind (denature) and join together loosely with their neighboring denatured proteins. Water between the proteins or attached to the proteins is held in a moist, tender network. If the water is too hot or the cooking time too long, the protein mesh tightens, squeezing out the water, and the proteins become tough.

You want to start in boiling water, which will set the outside fast, but then turn down the heat to maintain a low simmer for tender eggs. For very tender eggs, cover, simmer briefly, then remove them from the heat and let stand, covered, to allow the eggs to finish cooking. Also, a heavy nonstick pan will make the eggs less likely to stick.

You can poach eggs ahead. When the white is cooked, lift the eggs from the poaching water and place in a bowl of ice water. This will stop the cooking while the white is cooked but the yolk is still runny. Store them in the ice water in the refrigerator. When you are ready to serve, you can place them in a strainer a few at a time and lower them into simmering water for about forty-five seconds. Drain and serve immediately.

To poach 4 eggs, fill a nonstick 8-inch skillet a little over halfway with water (about 2 cups), add 2 teaspoons vinegar and ¾ teaspoon salt, and bring to a slow boil. Break an egg into a saucer and slip it into the water; repeat with the remaining eggs. (If you want to poach more than 4 eggs, use a larger skillet and arrange the eggs in a clockwise pattern so you will know which ones you put in first.) Just as the water comes back to a boil, reduce the heat to maintain a low simmer. When the eggs begin to set, take a spatula and gently run it under each one to release it from the bottom. If a yolk breaks, do not disturb it; it will seal by itself. Cook until the whites are firm, then lift the eggs out with a slotted spoon. Rinse them briefly in hot water to remove the vinegar. Drain well and serve.

You may have noticed the pretty teardrop shape of some restaurant-poached eggs. This is the shape formed as the egg gently sinks to the bottom of a tall pot of simmering water.

Many people love poached eggs. However, the USDA recommends fully cooking eggs because both the yolk and the white can be infected with salmonella. This is especially dangerous for at-risk populations, such as the very young or old, pregnant women, and people with weakened immunity.

For Great Poached Eggs	
What to Do	**Why**
Use very fresh eggs (grade AA, if possible).	The white of a fresh egg is thick and holds together. A fresh egg's yolk sack is strong and will not break easily.
Start in boiling water, then reduce the heat to maintain a low simmer, or cover and remove from the heat.	Boiling water will set the outside of the egg and prevent the white from spreading. Low heat will produce a tender egg.
Use vinegar and salt in the water.	Both acid (vinegar) and salt make the white of the egg cook (coagulate) faster so it does not spread.
When preparing poached eggs ahead, plunge the eggs into ice water after poaching, store in the ice water in the refrigerator, and reheat by lowering the eggs into simmering water briefly.	Ice water stops the cooking so that the white is cooked but the yolk is runny. The ice water and water for reheating also remove vinegar.
Use a heavy nonstick pan.	Eggs are less likely to stick.

UNSCRAMBLING SCRAMBLED EGGS

Eggs are liquid protein, which can seep into any imperfection in a pan. Heating an empty pan first—not to smoking hot, but just hot enough—will cause the metal to expand and seal imperfections in the pan's surface. When you pour the eggs in, they will cook on the surface, not in it.

A heavy nonstick skillet is a big help. Heat it gently first, spray lightly with nonstick cooking spray, return it to the heat for a few seconds, then add the beaten eggs. Let them sit, untouched, for a full minute and they will puff magnificently. The eggs hold on to trapped air, which expands when heated. If you stir the eggs vigorously immediately after they go into the pan, you'll stir all the air out of them and end up with small curds and not much volume.

After the eggs have puffed, gently push one edge to the center to allow the uncooked eggs to flow onto the bare pan. Do this until no liquid egg flows to the edge and you have a pan of soft mounds that still look slightly moist. By following these tips, you'll have soft, fluffy scrambled eggs, not tough, watery ones.

HARD-COOKED EGGS

Many people say hard-boiled eggs, but experts tell us we should not boil eggs, since it makes them tough. So, to emphasize this, the eggs are termed "hard-cooked." I arrange my eggs in one layer and add cold water to cover them by 1½ inches. I partially cover the pot, and when the water has reached a full rolling boil, I turn the heat down to low, completely cover the pan, and let the eggs cook for 1 minute. Then I remove them from the heat and let them sit in the hot water for 15 minutes. I then put them in a bowl of heavily iced water for 5 minutes to prevent overcooking.

The longer eggs are cooked, the more time iron in the yolk and sulfur in the white have to combine, which forms a compound that tints the yolks green. To avoid the green tinge, watch the cooking time carefully and rinse in cold water to stop the cooking.

Very fresh eggs are less alkaline and extremely difficult to peel. Eggs become more alkaline as they age and are therefore easier to peel. Eggs seven to ten days old should peel easily.

WHITES AND YOLKS

When to Use Whites

Use egg whites to dry. In baking, egg whites help make things like cream puffs dry and crisp. This can be a drawback in dishes that you want to be moist, like cakes and muffins. To moisten cakes or muffins, substitute 2 egg yolks for a whole egg.

Use egg whites for puff. For beautiful puffed toppings, use egg whites or an ingredient that contains eggs, like mayonnaise.

Use egg whites for light, nongreasy products when deep-frying, either in batter coatings or for noncoated dishes like fritters. Egg yolks absorb grease. Replacing some whole eggs with egg whites will lighten and dry your product.

When to Use Yolks

Use egg yolks for sensuously smooth textures and to add moisture. Natural emulsifiers in egg yolks hold fat and water together in many foods, including sauces like hollandaise, béarnaise, and mayonnaise. These emulsifiers are the secret to the creamy, satiny smooth texture in everything from chocolate truffles to custards. When you need less puff, yolks are ideal.

CUSTARDS

Another great way to cook eggs is in custards, but people seem to run into a lot of problems. Here are some tips for common complaints.

Custard Doesn't Set

You need more than 1 egg per cup of liquid for a barely set custard. For a quiche made with 2 cups of liquid, 3 eggs or 2 eggs plus 2 yolks would make a good custard.

A Skin Forms on the Surface

Casein from the dairy products in the sauce dries out on the surface, creating a skin (like the skin on hot chocolate). If you remove the skin, a new one will form. Press plastic wrap directly against the surface of the warm custard or sauce, or touch the end of a stick of butter to the hot surface to form a thin coating of fat across the pan. Either of these procedures prevents air from getting to the casein.

Thins When You Stir in Flavoring

Once a starch gel has cooled and set, any stirring will thin the custard. Stir in the vanilla, Grand Marnier, etc., while the custard is still hot and not firmly set.

Thins upon Standing Overnight in the Refrigerator

After egg yolks are added, pastry cream must be brought back to a boil to kill enzymes in the yolks that damage starch and cause thinning. This may be difficult because the custard may be thick and going *blop-blop*, but you must get the entire pastry cream above 170°F to kill all the enzymes. I scrape the bottom with a flat-ended spatula to prevent burning.

EGG WHITE FOAMS
(MERINGUES AND SOUFFLÉS)

For a confection with so few ingredients—just egg whites, sugar, and perhaps a pinch of acid like cream of tartar—meringues are surprisingly versatile and complex creatures. They can be hard, crisp shells (like vacherins) or cake layers (like dacquoise), or they can be soft, cloudlike toppings for pies and tarts. Meringues can also be troublemakers. They can weep, they can bead, and they can be too soft. As any pastry chef knows, making a light, stable egg white foam—the basic component of a meringue—is no simple matter.

What Is a Meringue?

A meringue is simply a mixture of beaten egg whites whipped with sugar until its volume increases and peaks form. Egg whites have a superb capacity to foam; as long as certain precautions are taken, they can increase in volume by up to eight times.

The first step in making meringue—beating air into egg whites—causes one of the egg white proteins, conalbumin,

71

to unwind (or denature). The unwound proteins link loosely together around the air bubbles, establishing a foam.

The key during this initial step is to beat the egg whites just until the proteins are loosely linked, which a pastry chef recognizes as the soft-peak stage. These loosely linked proteins allow the air bubbles to expand when they're heated so the soft meringue can rise until the heat sets all the proteins.

If the egg white foam is overbeaten, however, the protein bonds will tighten and the foam will set even before it gets heated. Then, when it is heated, the foam won't puff at all in the oven. If the beaten egg whites start to look at all dry, hard, or lumpy, they're probably overbeaten.

The Right Amount of Sugar

Sugar is a vital part of meringues. Besides adding sweetness, sugar helps stabilize the meringue's structure. When sugar is beaten into an egg white foam, it dissolves in the protein film on the surface of the air bubbles. This sugary syrup prevents the proteins from drying out and tightening up too fast.

Once you add sugar, you can beat the egg whites without worrying too much about them getting lumpy or overbeaten. But at the same time, sugar dramatically increases the beating time required to get good volume. Pastry chefs deal with this double-edged sword in different ways: some chefs add sugar to the whites in the beginning, turn the mixer on, and walk away, but most prefer to get some volume and structure in the whites first and then start adding the sugar.

The proportion of sugar to egg whites determines the meringue's texture. When you beat sugar into egg whites, the sugar draws water out of the whites. Then, when the meringue is heated (either in the oven—French meringue—or by pouring in a boiling sugar syrup—Italian meringue), the heat evaporates the water from the sugar syrup–encased air bubbles, and you end up with delicate, sugar-crusted bubbles.

The more sugar there is in a meringue, the more water can be drawn out and evaporated, and the drier and stiffer the meringue will be. In general, hard meringues require a ¼ cup of sugar per large egg white. For soft meringues, the traditional formula is 2 tablespoons sugar per egg white.

A meringue that's too soft or that can't hold its shape may simply not have enough sugar. For their cookbooks on healthful eating, Time-Life chefs found that they needed at least 1½ tablespoons of sugar per egg white to get a stable meringue.

Meringue Maladies

Meringues can be tricky, but with a little kitchen science, we can solve any issues.

Three common problems that occur with meringues are weeping, when "tears" of liquid collect in a puddle under the meringue; beading, when brown droplets of syrup form on the outer surface of the meringue; and shrinking, the tightening of the egg white proteins.

Weeping is caused by undercooking. If the proteins don't get hot enough to cook (or firmly set) the foam, it collapses, and the liquid film on the surface leaks out. If a soft meringue on a pie starts to weep after the meringue is baked, the meringue didn't get hot enough to cook all the way through. Prepare the meringue first (once the sugar has been beaten in, it is safe to sit for a while) and then make the filling so you can spoon the meringue onto a hot filling. It helps to pile the meringue onto a piping-hot pie rather than onto a chilled one. Another trick, gleaned from Roland Mesnier, a former White House pastry chef, is to sprinkle fine cake crumbs (nothing fancy—I've even used Twinkies) on top of the hot filling before mounding on the meringue. The combination of crumbs and hot filling gives you an incredibly dry seal between the meringue and the filling (the crumbs absorb any excess moisture and the heat from the pie helps cook the meringue from the bottom up).

Lowering the oven temperature and increasing the cooking time can help with weeping, too. Food reaches higher temperatures in the center when cooked at lower temperatures for a longer time. So to get my nine-egg-white-high meringue cooked through, I cook it at a fairly low temperature—300°F to 325°F—for 30 to 45 minutes.

For soft meringues that aren't baked but are just heated by a boiling sugar syrup (known as Italian meringues), weeping could be a result of the sugar syrup not being hot enough to fully "cook" the meringue.

Beading is caused by overcooking. The proteins tighten and squeeze out water droplets, which brown because of the sugar they contain. Try lowering the oven temperature or decreasing the baking time, or both, to solve this problem.

Shrinking can occur when meringues are baked in the oven. The tightening of the egg white proteins causes the meringue to shrink, and also makes the meringue difficult to cut smoothly. My solution to this problem is to add a little cornstarch paste to the meringue. Cornstarch prevents the egg white bonds from tightening (in the same way that it prevents eggs from curdling in a pastry cream) so the meringue doesn't shrink. This tender meringue with starch cuts like a dream.

To add cornstarch to a meringue, first dissolve the cornstarch in water (dry cornstarch can't access the water in the meringue) and heat it. Dissolve 1 tablespoon of cornstarch in ⅓ cup of water and heat it until a thick paste forms. After all the sugar is beaten into the egg whites and the meringue is firm, keep the mixer running and add the cornstarch paste, a teaspoon at a time.

SOUFFLÉS

If your soufflé does not rise, the egg white foam was probably overbeaten so the protein network was "cooked" and not soft and elastic and able to expand while cooking. Beat the whites until they still slip a little in the bowl.

PÂTE À CHOUX (CREAM PUFF) PROBLEMS

Puffs Do Not Rise

Heat must come from the bottom for puffs to rise well before the top crust forms. I preheat the oven to 450°F with a pizza stone in the lower third of the oven, getting the stone really hot, then lower the temperature to 425°F, leave the oven door open for 30 seconds to cool a little, then place the pâte à choux on the hot stone to cook. Bake for 15 minutes to puff them well, then turn the temperature down to 325°F for about 20 minutes more to dry them out well—these are times for small puffs; regular cream puffs will take longer to cook. Also, for the best—higher, crisper—puffs, use 2 whole eggs and the rest whites.

Puffs Fall after Removing from the Oven

Puffs must be thoroughly dried out or they will fall. Turn the oven temperature down (to about 75°F to 100°F) when puffs are brown and leave them in to dry out well. When they are removed from the oven, cut small slits in the sides of the puffs to allow steam to escape.

Puffs Have Gooey, Undercooked Centers

Egg whites are excellent drying agents. For drier puffs, use only 1 or 2 whole eggs and use whites for the rest of the needed liquid in the standard 4-egg recipe.

EVERYTHING MATTERS
WHEN MAKING MERINGUES

Condition of the Eggs

Room-temperature whites whip faster than cold ones. Old egg whites whip faster, and to a slightly greater volume, but fresh whites make a more stable foam that holds up better during cooking.

Pure Whites

Fats destroy egg white foams, and egg yolks and olive oil are two of the most destructive. One tiny smidge of yolk in the whites, or of grease on the beaters or bowl, can give you a thick, gray mess rather than a light, stable foam.

Type of Sugar

For soft meringues, superfine sugar (also called bar or caster sugar) is preferable because it dissolves faster. For hard meringues, confectioners' sugar will give a lighter result.

Type of Bowl

A copper bowl is best; a plastic bowl is worst. Beating whites in a copper bowl helps increase the volume during baking. Avoid plastic, which is difficult to rid of trace amounts of fat.

Type of Whisk

For hand beating, use a balloon whisk with many tines—more tines incorporate more air faster. If using an electric hand mixer, be sure to move the beaters around in the bowl.

How Long to Beat

Beat the whites first to soft peaks. Then add the sugar gradually while beating and beat until the whites are firm enough to hold detailed swirls. It's imperative that you beat the meringue until it's very firm.

CHEESE

Cooking with cheese can have an occasional surprising result. The biggest problems: curdling and stringiness. But never fear; science is here to help you avoid these cooking mishaps.

Cheese is made by curdling milk with an enzyme (rennet), or with heat, or both. When we're dealing with curds, it shouldn't come as a surprise that further curdling can occur.

The natural proteins in cheese are individual units, like little wads of string. They float around totally separated. When you heat these proteins, or add acid—or, with some, just expose them to air—bonds in the wadded-up protein release and partially unwind. Almost immediately, an unwound protein with its bonds sticking out will run into another unwound protein, and they will join together. Initially, when these proteins bond, they are moist and tender, because a lot of water is trapped between them. But if you continue to heat them, the bonds tighten and squeeze out the moisture, making the proteins dry and tough. Because the proteins in cheese are already linked, they can easily overcook and curdle. Many recipes tell you to remove the dish from the heat and then stir in the grated cheese. This helps you avoid the overheating that can cause curdling.

Cheese sauces that contain starch also help us avoid curdling: a dish that has a little starch such as flour in the sauce won't curdle, whereas one that contains only grated cheese and milk may.

This leaves us with the battle against stringy cheese. If you stir a cheese sauce for very long after the cheese is added, it may become stringy. Many cooks would not dream of putting mozzarella into a sauce because of this problem. The reason: mozzarella and other cheeses, including Swiss, contain calcium phosphate, which can link cheese proteins together to form long strings.

To reduce this, cooks have traditionally added dry white wine to such cheese dishes as fondue. Wine contains tartaric acid, which helps prevent calcium phosphate from linking the proteins. But the citric acid in lemon juice is even more effective; it binds with calcium and can overcome stringiness even in mozzarella.

I love to make fettuccine with a sauce of mozzarella and prosciutto or country ham. To prevent it from becoming stringy, I sprinkle a little lemon juice on the grated cheese, then stir it into the cream sauce over low heat. You will be astounded at how well this works.

FETTUCCINE WITH MOZZARELLA, HAM, MUSHROOMS, AND TOMATOES

A luscious creamy cheese sauce over pasta with ham, mushroom, and tomatoes—a great pasta dish!

What This Recipe Shows

Butter, oil, and cheese carry fat-soluble flavors.

Mushrooms, cheese, ham, and tomatoes trigger umami taste receptors eight times due to synergism.

Lemon juice on grated cheese prevents stringiness for a creamy sauce.

¼ cup dried mushrooms, such as cèpes or porcini
⅓ cup hot water
1 tablespoon plus ½ teaspoon finely ground sea salt
2 tablespoons butter
3 tablespoons flour

⅛ teaspoon ground pepper

1 teaspoon sugar

2 cups whole milk or half-and-half

2 tablespoons fresh lemon juice

¾ cup grated mozzarella cheese

½ teaspoon red pepper flakes

¼ cup olive oil

¾ cup chopped country ham or prosciutto

8 ounces fresh mushrooms, sliced

4 tomatoes, peeled, seeded, and coarsely chopped,
   or 1 (28 ounce) can diced tomatoes, well drained

18 ounces fettuccine

In a small bowl, soak the dried mushrooms in the hot water to soften. Set aside.

Bring a gallon of water with 1 tablespoon of the salt added to a boil. Meanwhile, in a large skillet, melt the butter over medium heat. Stir in the flour, the remaining ½ teaspoon salt, pepper, and sugar; simmer on low for 2 minutes. Remove from the heat and whisk in the milk. Cook over medium heat, stirring constantly, until smooth.

Sprinkle the lemon juice over the mozzarella and toss to coat. Whisk the cheese into the sauce.

In a large skillet over medium heat, stir the red pepper flakes into the olive oil. Stir in the ham and fresh mushrooms. Sauté briefly and remove from the heat. Remove the dried mushrooms from their soaking water with a slotted spoon and add them to the skillet. Pour all but the last tablespoon of the soaking liquid (which may contain sand) into the skillet. Stir

the ham-mushroom mixture and the tomatoes into the mozzarella sauce.

Add the fettuccine to the boiling water. Cook for the time
recommended on the package. Stir for the first 2 minutes of
cooking. Drain the pasta and add it to the skillet with the
cheese sauce. Cover and let stand for 1 minute. Serve hot.

Makes 6 servings

SWEET AND SAVORY
CHEESCAKES 101

Cheesecakes are custards that happen to be made with cream
cheese instead of milk. Sweet dessert cheesecakes typically
come to mind first, but savory cheesecakes make excellent
hors d'oeuvres for large parties. On a pedestal cake dish, an
herbed cheesecake encircled with fresh herbs or herb blos-
soms is dramatic. It can be cut wedding cake–style—a circle
cut about 1½ inches from the outside, then ½-inch slices cut
but not removed—so that guests can easily serve themselves a
small rectangular piece.

Like custards, there are two major categories of cheesecakes—those without starch and those with starch (usually
a few tablespoons of flour or cornstarch). Cheesecakes and
other egg-thickened dishes have a different texture when
starch is added. The amount of starch added determines the
extent of the textural change. The addition of one tablespoon
of flour creates a small but noticeable difference, while several
tablespoons of starch make a significant textural difference.

CHEESECAKES WITHOUT STARCH

Like custards without starch (crème anglaise, stirred custard), cheesecakes without starch must be cooked at lower temperatures to prevent the eggs from curdling. They can be cooked in a 275°F oven. Betsy Murelle, a cookware shop owner and outstanding cook, bakes her cheesecakes in a 275°F oven for one hour, then leaves them in the turned-off oven for another hour.

Many cooks like to use a water bath, which keeps the temperature around 200°F in a 350°F oven. My friend Doris Koplin, a professional baker and cheesecake expert, makes hers without starch and bakes them in a 350°F oven for 30 minutes to get the cake hot, then turns off the oven and leaves the cheesecakes in the closed, cooling oven for about an hour to continue cooking very slowly.

If you are using a springform pan in a water bath, you need to double wrap the outside of the pan with aluminum foil to prevent water from seeping in. Even though you have to invert the cheesecake twice, I prefer using a 2- or 3-inch high cake pan, depending on the depth of the cheesecake.

The crumb/butter crust can stick to the bottom of the pan, so I soften the butter just enough for it to release easily by heating the bottom of the pan on a burner on the stove for a few seconds before unmolding the cheesecake. I invert it first onto a flat baking sheet covered with waxed paper, then I reinvert it onto a cake board or directly onto a pedestal cake dish so that it is right-side up.

The texture of a cheesecake without starch is quite smooth, and if the cake contains 2 to 3 cups of heavy cream or sour cream, the texture is incredibly creamy—a sensuous, luxurious texture for a rich dessert cheesecake.

CHEESECAKES WITH STARCH

When you add starch—even just 2 or 3 tablespoons of flour—to a cheesecake, you change the texture and the method of preparation. With the starch present, there is no danger of the eggs coagulating, so you can safely cook the cheesecake at a higher temperature—325°F is just fine.

If you think back to the two types of custards, crème anglaise (or stirred custard) is made with flavored milk or cream, sugar, and eggs (no starch) and must be prepared in a double boiler and stirred constantly to keep the heat even. If you heat it to more than 180°F, you get scrambled eggs and pale yellow liquid.

On the other hand, pastry cream (crème pâtissière) has essentially, the same ingredients—flavored milk or cream, sugar and eggs—but also a little starch (usually flour or cornstarch). This custard is prepared over direct medium-low heat with constant stirring. There is no danger of the eggs scrambling, and it thickens beautifully as it comes to a low boil. Just as the methods of preparation are different, the textures of the two custards are completely different.

Depending on how much starch is in the recipe, the cheesecake will be coarser with a totally different texture than the satiny smooth starchless cheesecakes. This coarser texture is, however, ideal for a savory herbed cheesecake (see *BakeWise*, pages 341–42).

When you are mixing the cheesecake, it is important to get

all the lumps out of the cream cheese and then blend in the eggs one at a time. If you add the eggs all at once before you have gotten all the lumps out of the cream cheese, the lumps simply float around in the excess liquid and you cannot beat them out.

WHY CHEESECAKES CRACK

The most frequent question that I get about cheesecakes is: "Why did my cheesecake crack?" It is always difficult for cooks to believe the answer, but cheesecakes crack because they are overcooked. I usually get a violent protest. "That can't be. The center of the cheesecake jiggled like it was not done." That observation is true. While the cheesecake is hot, the center shakes as if it is not done, but when it is cold, examine that center around the crack. It is firm and dry—overcooked.

The doneness of a cheesecake is one of the most deceptive things in cooking. I have made Rose Levy Beranbaum's cheesecake in all sizes and forms—plain cheesecakes, wedding cake cheesecakes, etc. I know I have made it at least 50 times and yet every time, I think it really isn't done—something must have gone wrong. There is an area in the center of the cheesecake at least 3 inches in diameter that jiggles like it is totally runny. I have to force myself to put the cake in the refrigerator. All my culinary instincts are screaming that it is not done. But, amazingly, when it is chilled, the cheesecake is perfectly cooked.

My friend Doris, the professional baker, says that occasionally she may be on the phone and not hear the timer so she accidentally overcooks her cheesecakes and, of course, they crack. She fills the cracks with whipped cream and ices the cheesecake with whipped cream and no one ever knows.

The recipe itself has some influence on the cooking time and the likelihood of cracking. The less sugar or more eggs in the recipe, the greater the chances of overcooking. You may want to try increasing the sugar a little and/or cutting one egg out of the recipe. The simplest way to avoid cracks is to reduce the cooking time. There are many recipes out there with incorrect cooking directions. I like the procedure of leaving the cake in the turned-off oven to finish cooking. For more information on cheesecakes, see the recipes in *BakeWise*, pages 333–34 and pages 341–42.

Cooking Times That Work

For Cheesecakes Without Starch

275°F for 1 hour, turn the oven off, leave in the oven for 1 hour

350°F in a water bath for 45 minutes, turn the oven off, leave in the oven for 1 hour

350°F for 30 minutes, turn the oven off, leave in the oven for 1 hour

For Cheesecakes with Starch

325°F for 50 minutes to 1 hour

CHAPTER THREE

VEGETABLES AND FRUITS

Plants are not only our food supply, they also take in the carbon dioxide that animals produce and turn it into oxygen.

Learning the best ways to care for and use plant products—our precious fruits and vegetables—can make our meals more delicious.

STORAGE

"Don't look now, but your lettuce is breathing."

Fruits and vegetables are plant parts. Even when they are removed from the plant, their cells are still alive and conducting living processes. Their cells take in oxygen, use it to break up big chemicals, and give off carbon dioxide, just as our cells do.

If your lettuce is gasping, it's deteriorating fast. To keep lettuce in good shape longer, you have to cut off its oxygen! Lettuce can keep for over a month in the refrigerator if it is washed, spun dry, and sealed in heavy-duty zip-top plastic freezer bags. The storage problem is magnified with delicate vegetables like lettuce, but the principles hold for other fruits and vegetables.

For better produce storage, we have to fight moisture loss, mold growth, and natural deterioration.

In *On Food and Cooking*, Harold McGee points out that fruits and vegetables are pretty wrappers for water. Some, like lettuce, are 96 percent water. Even lower moisture potatoes are 84 percent water. Commercially, markets use "rain" on delicate produce like lettuce that becomes wilted with only 4 percent water loss. Produce storage areas are held at high humidity, and citrus fruits, cucumbers, turnips, and others are coated with wax to limit water loss. Some produce like celery is sold in plastic wrap to limit loss. Now we have everything from lettuce to chopped slaw mix washed, dried, and sealed in bags containing inert gases to keep oxygen out.

Surface moisture provides good conditions for mold growth—the dreaded brown slime. To reduce mold growth, remove as much surface water as possible with a salad spinner. Or I like to put my lettuce in a clean pillowcase, step out the back door, and spin it around my head.

Reducing the temperature through refrigeration is a major step in slowing metabolism. Dr. Robert Shewfelt, an expert on produce quality, says immediate refrigeration greatly enhances produce quality and life. Reducing oxygen is also a great way to slow metabolism. I was stunned by how long I could keep lettuce refrigerated by squeezing out the air and tightly sealing in zip-top freezer bags.

Many of the new top-of-the-line refrigerators do an excellent job of increasing produce storage time with crisper drawers that are humidity controlled and limit air flow to control both moisture loss and oxygen availability.

Enzymatic Browning

When fruit is cut or bruised, it browns, a process called enzymatic browning. This is a reaction (enhanced by enzymes) of phenolic compounds in the fruit with oxygen in the air. To avoid this, you can either prevent oxygen from touching the surface by covering with a nonpermeable plastic wrap (such as Saran Wrap) or by coating the fruit with some form of vitamin C (which slows this reaction). Many cooks use lemon juice. Orange juice is just as effective and doesn't interfere with the taste of delicate foods.

COOKING

Fresh fruits and vegetables are made of living, breathing cells. With heat from any source, regardless of the cooking method, plant cells die and experience dramatic changes. Heat immediately denatures the cell membranes that control the flow of water in and out of the cells. The cells lose water and become limp even if they are cooked in water.

The insoluble pectic substances that provided rigid support between the cells convert into water-soluble pectins. Everything but the cellulose and lignin in the cell walls softens. Once this glue (the pectic substances) between the cell walls is converted to pectins and dissolves, the cells start to separate. They shrink as the proteins coagulate; they rupture and leak and lose water, and they fall apart. It's no wonder that fruits and vegetables soften when they are cooked!

With this mass destruction of the cells, there are many chemical changes. Compounds with low boiling points boil off. Some compounds break down and some combine to create new substances with different tastes.

Sugar and calcium prevent the change in pectic substances and preserve the glue between the cells. You can see this dramatically in the difference between refried beans and Boston baked beans. If you cook navy or pinto beans for 4 to 6 hours, they become mush—looking like refried beans. But, if you cook the same beans with brown sugar and molasses, which has both sugar and calcium, they retain their shape after cooking all day and become Boston baked beans. Cooks can use sugar and/or calcium as tools to preserve shape. A cook may sauté apple wedges until they are as soft as she would like, then add sugar to preserve the texture. In the following Golden Carrots recipe, I was careful to cook the carrots to soften first and then added sugar to preserve their shape.

Water Loss

As discussed in chapter one on flavor, when water is lost, flavors become more intense. This can be a small water loss as in brief steaming or boiling of vegetables, or an extensive water loss as in drying. In roasting, the liquid that comes out of the damaged vegetable cells immediately evaporates and concentrates the flavor. Long roasting of vegetables like onions and root vegetables caramelizes their exterior, giving them more complex sweet tastes.

COOKING TIME

Green vegetables profit from quick cooking. There are two forms of chlorophyll—beautiful bright green and yucky army drab. When you heat green vegetables, their cell walls shrink and acids in the cells leak out, causing discoloration of the bright green. Whether you boil, steam, broil, or grill, a short cooking time is the key to retaining the bright color.

Raw green vegetables will hold their color in acidic dressings because of their natural waterproof coating; however, raw vegetables are not as bright in color because of the fine air bubbles that coat their surface. When you blanch raw vegetables, they become brighter in color because the fine bubbles have popped. But the vegetable surface will now be exposed to acid.

Green beans get tender 10 percent faster when cooked in salted water. Green beans cooked in salted boiling water for less than 7 minutes and then rinsed to stop the cooking and remove the salt will be bright green. You can reheat them briefly with a little butter when you are ready to serve them. Broccoli florets cooked in the same manner for 5 minutes or less will be a beautiful green. Notice the short cooking time in the asparagus recipe that follows.

A short cooking time is the secret to a sweet, mild flavor with members of the cabbage family. Between 5 and 7 minutes of cooking time, the foul-smelling hydrogen sulfide compounds in cabbage double. If you slice cabbage very thinly, as you would for cole slaw, and cook it for 5 minutes or less, it will be a tender, mild, wonderful-flavored vegetable.

Here are a few of my all-time favorite vegetable recipes.

FOUR-MINUTE ASPARAGUS

Perfectly cooked, gorgeous, bright green asparagus are ready in minutes. An ideal side for any meal, this delicious dish conjures simple elegance.

What This Recipe Shows

Short cooking time keeps the chlorophyll bright green.

Sugar helps the asparagus retain its shape.

Lemon zest adds zippy lemon flavor without turning the asparagus a yucky, army drab green, as lemon juice would.

---

1 pound fresh asparagus, rinsed in cold water
3 tablespoons olive oil
½ teaspoon fine sea salt
½ teaspoon sugar
Zest of 1 lemon

Preheat the broiler.

With one hand at the root end of an asparagus stalk and the other hand three-quarters of the way up the stalk, gently bend until the stalk breaks. The asparagus will snap where the tough portion ends. Repeat with all the asparagus.

Spread out the asparagus on a baking sheet. Drizzle with the oil and then roll the asparagus to coat all sides.

Slip the pan under the broiler, 6 or 7 inches from the heat source, and broil for 4 minutes only. Sprinkle the asparagus with the salt, sugar, and lemon zest and place on a serving platter or individual plates. Serve hot, cold, or at room temperature.

Makes 4 to 6 servings

FINE CABBAGE SHREDS WITH CREAM

Cabbage cooked briefly has fascinating, subtle, sweet flavors. This is a quick, easy dish that is surprisingly delicious.

What This Recipe Shows

Slicing cabbage very thinly allows it to get tender in a short cooking time.

A short cooking time omits off-flavor compounds.

1 small head cabbage
½ cup heavy cream or half and half
1½ tablespoons finely ground sea salt
1 teaspoon sugar

Cut the cabbage in half and place each half, cut-side down, on a cutting board. Slice the cabbage into very thin shreds.

In a large skillet, add the cream. Gently bring to a simmer, then adjust the heat to keep the cream just below a simmer and cook until it begins to thicken. Remove from the heat and set aside.

Bring a medium pot of water with the salt to a boil. Add the cabbage. Cook for 4 to 5 minutes only. Drain well. Stir the cabbage into the skillet with the cream and add the sugar. Stir well. Reheat and serve.

Makes 4 servings

GOLDEN CARROTS

A way to make cooking easier is to take advantage of packaged peeled and cut fresh vegetables. My market has packaged fresh carrots trimmed into matchsticks or ruffled slices, as well as baby carrots. Whole carrots peeled and chopped into pieces work well also.

Brown sugar is magic with carrots. These are so good that children don't realize that they are eating carrots. I use a little orange marmalade (which contains orange zest) to provide the zippy flavor of orange zest. If you like foods really spicy hot, you can add ½ teaspoon cayenne pepper when you add the brown sugar.

½ teaspoon finely ground sea salt

1 cup water

2 bags 10-ounce matchstick-cut fresh carrots

3 tablespoons butter

2 tablespoons dark brown sugar

2 tablespoons orange marmalade, or 1 tablespoon
    orange zest

In a large skillet, combine the salt and water and bring to a boil. Add the carrots. Turn down the heat to maintain a low simmer, cover, and cook for about 5 minutes, until the carrots are tender. Remove the cover; turn the heat up and cook, stirring occasionally, to evaporate most of the water.

Stir in the butter, brown sugar, and orange marmalade. Stir well to coat all the carrots. Serve hot or at room temperature. For a lighter version, this is also delicious with ½ tablespoon each of butter, sugar, and marmalade.

Makes about 6 servings

DOES COOKING BOOST OR BUST NUTRIENTS IN VEGETABLES?

Which do you think delivers more nutrients—a raw carrot or a cooked one? If you're like most people, you'd probably pick the raw one. And you'd be wrong. Contrary to popular belief, some vegetables actually benefit nutritionally from cooking. It's also true that cooking can destroy certain nutrients. And you might be surprised to learn that in some cases, cooking doesn't make that much of a difference at all.

Salads and fresh vegetable dishes are of course wonderfully healthy, but when I hear about people who adamantly eat only raw vegetables, I get worried. Some vegetables actually become more nutritious after cooking. For carrots, cooking softens their firm cell structure—we can access many more carotenes, minerals, and vitamin C in tender cooked carrots than we can by simply chewing raw, crunchy ones.

Corn is another example of how cooking can unlock nutrients. Corn contains lysine, one of the essential amino acids (which are the building blocks of proteins), but it's in a form that our bodies can't use. By cooking corn with a strong alkali (such as ashes, burnt shells, lye, or limestone), as some cultures that lived predominantly on corn did, the lysine converts to a usable form. Today, we get our lysine from other food sources.

Another generally unrecognized fact is that the nutrient content of a particular kind of vegetable (or fruit) can vary immensely. One grapefruit can contain two hundred times more vitamin A than another. Genetic differences among varieties account for some of this range, but growing conditions, the time of harvest, and handling and storage conditions are also factors. For example, snap beans build up their stash of vitamin C and carrots develop more beta-carotene as they mature. Some produce, such as spinach, can lose up to half its total vitamin C in twenty-four hours after harvest if it isn't refrigerated. So be aware that even before you've settled on whether to steam or sauté, some significant nutrient loss may have already occurred.

How to Preserve the Most Nutrients During Cooking

So how much nutrient damage really occurs when you boil or steam or sauté or roast vegetables? It's difficult to say exactly, but the differences among various cooking methods aren't as great as you might think. For minerals like iron, calcium, magnesium, potassium, and sodium, the loss is only in the range of 5 to 10 percent no matter how the vegetable is cooked. Vitamin loss, on the other hand, can be much higher, although many vegetables (such as tomatoes, eggplant, asparagus, and green beans) retain 80 percent or more of their vitamins regardless of the cooking method.

Nutrients escape from vegetables in two ways: by getting dissolved in the cooking water or by getting destroyed by heat.

Water-soluble compounds (which include vitamin C and some B vitamins) are the most vulnerable to boiling, simmering, steaming, or braising. The simplest way to minimize the loss of these nutrients is to choose a cooking method that doesn't involve water, or to cook vegetables in a way that the cooking liquid remains part of the dish, as it does in a casserole or a braise.

Again, for minerals, the loss is only in the range of 5 to 10 percent no matter how the vegetable is cooked.

When you do choose to boil vegetables, adding them to the water after it has come to a full boil (as you would when blanching) minimizes the loss of vitamin C. If you start them in cold or warm water, enzymes in the vegetables become very active—at boiling temperatures, the enzymes are deactivated. Some of these enzymes are major destroyers of vitamin C, eliminating 20 percent of the vitamin within the first two minutes of cooking. Since blanching is a better way to cook many green vegetables, this method works quite well.

Another way to moderately limit nutrient loss is to steam vegetables in a minimum of water with a lid, which reduces the loss of water-soluble vitamins and volatile nutrients. But be aware that the crisp green color of some vegetables will become drab, and vegetables from the brassica family (broccoli, cabbage, and cauliflower, for example) will become strong tasting if cooked for a longer time.

Rapid cooking can help preserve some thiamine and vitamin C, which are the most susceptible to destruction by heat. Stir-frying and sautéing, both fast-cooking methods, are good techniques for minimizing nutrient loss as well as for keeping green vegetables bright. Another tip is to cut vegetables into smaller pieces to reduce their cooking time.

Cooking has little detrimental effect on the nutritive value of carotenoids, which are the precursors to vitamin A found in orange and yellow vegetables like carrots, sweet potatoes, squash, and rutabagas. Carotenoids (beta-carotene is one example) are also found in red vegetables like red bell peppers and in dark green vegetables like broccoli and spinach. Studies suggest that cooking may even boost this nutrient in some cases.

Carotenoids deteriorate with lengthy exposure to oxygen. Dried carrot chips, for example, lose their beta-carotene when packaged in air—but retain it when packaged with nitrogen.

Whatever cooking method you choose, it's important to keep perspective. When it's time to start cooking, I think about food as more than just sustenance. For me, the decision of how to cook my vegetables includes things like flavor, appearance, time, and which method my family prefers. After all, it doesn't matter how nutritious your vegetables are if you can't get anyone to eat them!

QUICK ROAST POTATOES AND CARROTS

High-temperature roasting produces root vegetables that are a beautiful golden brown and delicious with a much shorter cooking time.

What This Recipe Shows

The high temperature caramelizes sugars on the vegetables' surface for great flavors and rich browning.

3 tablespoons olive oil with a high smoke point
4 medium Yukon Gold potatoes (about 1 pound), cut
    into ½- to ¾-inch cubes
1 large red onion (about 1 pound), coarsely chopped
½ pound baby carrots (about 1 cup), cut to match the
    size of the potatoes
1 large garlic clove, minced
½ teaspoon fine sea salt
6 green onions, white and a little of the green part,
    thinly sliced

Preheat the oven to 500°F.

In a 10 by 15-inch flameproof roasting pan or cast iron skillet, heat the oil over high heat for about 1 minute.

Add the potatoes, onion, and carrots and toss in the hot oil to coat well. Place the pan in the oven and roast for 10 minutes, then stir well and roast for 10 minutes more, stirring once. Keep an eye on the vegetables and remove from the heat if they are in danger of burning or are overdone. Test for doneness by sticking a fork or knife into a vegetable or two. Add the garlic and salt and toss well. Roast for 5 minutes more.

Place the vegetables on a serving platter, sprinkle with the green onions, and serve.

Makes 4 servings

FRUITS

A NOTE ON RIPENING

Only certain fruits get sweeter ripened when off the plant. Jeffrey Steingarten, in his excellent article on ripe fruit in *Vogue* magazine, divides fruits into five categories:

1) Fruits that never ripen after they are picked (blackberries, cacao, cherries, grapefruit, grapes, lemons, limes, lychee, mandarins, olives, oranges, pineapples, raspberries, strawberries, and watermelons).
2) Fruits that ripen only after picking (avocados).
3) Fruits that ripen in color, texture, and juiciness, but do not ripen in flavor or sweetness after harvest (apricots, blueberries, cantaloupes, casaba melons, crenshaws, figs, honeydews, nectarines, passion fruit, peaches, Persian melons, and persimmons).
4) Fruits that do get sweeter after harvest (apples, cherimoyas, kiwifruits, mangoes, papayas, pears, sapotes, and soursops).
5) Fruits that ripen in every way after harvest (bananas).

Bananas in a fruit arrangement get overripe overnight. Some fruits (like ripe apples and bananas) naturally give off ethylene gas, which speeds up ripening. Keep bananas away from apples to slow ripening. Use apples to speed the ripening of avocados: warm avocados by setting them in the sun or microwave them for twenty seconds, then place them in a paper bag with several apples, close the bag loosely, and leave at room temperature overnight.

Raw pineapple has an enzyme that will attack gelatin and muscle fiber. Raw ginger, figs, papayas, kiwifruits, and honeydews all contain enzymes that will wreck gelatin and sometimes muscle fiber, too.

HELPING MOTHER NATURE

Our first step toward magnificent fruit cookery is to recognize that with many fruits, it is up to us to finish Mother Nature's job of sweetening. It is not a sin to sweeten fresh fruit that was supposed to be sweet. Taste the fruit. If it is not sweet and wonderful, do something! Add sugar. I sometimes add a little fresh ginger for its crisp zip, too.

FRESH FRUIT WITH GINGER

A real eye-catching dish—bright-colored cold fresh fruit in a tall clear glass container. People go crazy over this dish. Some end up standing over the bowl, serving themselves, eating, and serving themselves again and again—sweet, juicy fresh fruit is so good!

What This Recipe Shows

The zippy flavor of ginger enhances the mild taste of fresh fruit.

1 (2-inch) piece fresh ginger, peeled and finely chopped

1 cup boiling water

1 cup sugar

2 cups cool water

⅛ teaspoon fine sea salt

3 seedless oranges, peeled and sliced

½ cantaloupe, peeled, seeded, and cut into chunks

2 cups hulled strawberries

2 cups black or red seedless grapes

In a small bowl, add the ginger and pour the boiling water over it, and allow to stand for about 25 minutes. Strain the liquid and discard the ginger. In a small saucepan, add the ginger water, sugar, cool water, and salt. Heat just to dissolve the sugar. Place the ginger-sugar water in the refrigerator to chill well. In a large bowl, combine the oranges, cantaloupe, strawberries, and grapes. Pour some or all of the ginger syrup over the fresh fruit. Cover with plastic wrap and refrigerate overnight before serving. I serve this dish in a tall clear glass container to show off the fruits' beauty.

Makes 5 to 6 servings

COOKING WITH FRUIT

How can we keep blueberries in a pie plump and beautiful, or strawberries in a dessert firm and pretty instead of smushed? When you heat fruits or vegetables, their cells fall apart and lose liquid. Heat causes the pectic substance (the glue that holds the cells together) to change to water-soluble pectins, which dissolve and cause the cells to fall apart. The fruit or vegetable softens and eventually collapses.

Even apples, which are firm, contain 86 percent water. When you heat fruits, they lose a lot of this water. This is why fruit pies or cobblers become watery and boil over during cooking.

So, we want to preserve the shape of the beautiful fruit and we want to prevent the fruits from watering down our dish. Two great experts have solutions for us: Monroe Boston Strause, known in the 1930s as the Pie King, and Roland Mesnier, who served as the White House pastry chef for many administrations.

In Strause's book, *Pie Marches On*, he offers a great solution. He carefully stirs the fruit (peeled and sliced when appropriate) with a portion of the sugar in the dish and allows this to stand in a colander over a bowl for at least 3 hours. This partially sweetens the fruit and draws out a considerable amount of water. This drained liquid (adjusted to 1 cup) can be reduced to concentrate the flavor and then thickened with tapioca flour (tapioca starch) (3 tablespoons stirred into ¼ cup water). When you bring the thickened juice to a boil, it will form a stiff paste. Stir to prevent scorching. I like to use a flat-ended wooden spatula so that I can scrape the bottom. Bringing the thickened juice to a boil causes changes in the starch so that it can no longer continue to thicken. When the pie is baked, this prevents the filling from becoming a thick, starchy mess. After the thickened juice comes to a boil, stir in the remaining sugar and the salt. The filling will thin. Bring this mixture back to a boil to evaporate some of the liquid until it thickens enough to coat the back of a spoon, again stirring to prevent scorching. Pour the cooked mixture over the drained fruit and carefully stir with a wooden spatula. Do not refrigerate the fruit mixture, but allow to cool before pouring it into the crust to bake. Fruit prepared this way retains its shape. The firm fruit's juices have been converted to a syrupy glaze that will not become cloudy. It has shine and luster. The fruit is not mashed up or broken, and the filling is just luscious, beautiful, delicious fruit.

Roland Mesnier solves the problem of keeping the fruit beautiful in cold desserts by making a strong sugar syrup (3 cups sugar and 1 cup water, brought to a boil). He keeps this syrup barely at a simmer, adds the fruit, and simmers for less than 15 minutes (simmering smaller fruits for less time, 1 to 2 minutes for blueberries). He lifts the fruit out to drain and boils down the fruit-sugar water until it is an intensely fruit-flavored syrup. He now has beautiful fruit and incredible syrup to flavor his dessert.

The following blueberries and bordeaux recipe is a very easy way to make a magnificent fresh blueberry pie. It is a major shortcut version of Mesnier's method of using sugar syrup to preserve fresh fruit's shape—just melt a little jelly! You will love this recipe. It, along with other great recipes, appears in my book *BakeWise*.

BORDEAUX-MACADAMIA CRUST

Delicious, sweeter-than-shortbread Bordeaux cookies combined with macadamia nuts make an incredible crust—perfect for cold fruit pies like my friend Judy Brady's Blueberries and Bordeaux (recipe follows), mousses or chiffon pies, or even cheesecakes! Even without additional sugar, the large amount of sugar in the cookies makes the crust uncuttable. To reduce the sugar concentration in the crumbs, I could have added bread crumbs, zwieback crumbs, or finely chopped nuts. But I selected macadamia nuts. To moisten the crust a little, I added some flaked coconut. Because of the richness of the macadamia nuts, I used less butter than in a plain graham cracker crumb crust.

What This Recipe Shows

Using cookies instead of graham cracker crumbs and sugar adds more flavors.

Finely chopped nuts cut the amount of sugar needed, making the crust easier to cut.

Nonstick spray
27 Pepperidge Farm Bordeaux cookies (a whole 6.75-ounce package)
½ to ¾ cup roasted salted macadamia nuts (about 3 ounces)
⅓ cup sweetened flaked coconut
3 tablespoons butter, melted

Place a shelf in the center of the oven and preheat the oven to 350°F. Spray a 9-inch pie pan with nonstick spray.

In a food processor, combine the cookies and nuts and process until broken down into fine crumbs. Add the coconut and pulse a few times to blend well. While pulsing, drizzle in the melted butter to combine.

Spread the crumb mixture around in the prepared pan and press it up the sides and across the bottom. Bake for about 8 minutes. Cool completely before filling.

Makes one 9-inch crust

JUDY BRADY'S BLUEBERRIES AND BORDEAUX

From my friend Judy Brady, a longtime great cook in Fort Walton Beach, Florida—fresh cold blueberries in a cookie crust. This is hard to beat—the perfect summertime dessert. And it is incredibly easy!

The teaspoon of gelatin called for in the recipe just sets the pie. A little juice will trickle from the slice. If you want a completely firm pie, use 1⅓ to 1½ teaspoons gelatin.

What This Recipe Shows

Sugar in the preserves maintains the shape of the blueberries.

Added gelatin will set the pie when cooled.

¼ cup cool water

1 teaspoon unflavored powdered gelatin

1 cup red or black seedless raspberry jam or blueberry preserves (about 11 ounces, maybe a whole small jar—I usually use Smuckers)

¼ teaspoon finely ground sea salt

5 to 6 cups fresh blueberries (a little less than 1½ quarts—I like it to be a full pie), very quickly rinsed in a colander and drained

1 Bordeaux-Macadamia Crust (see above), cooled

1 recipe Mascarpone Cream (recipe follows)

Pour the water into a glass measuring cup, sprinkle the gelatin over, and allow to soften.

In a medium saucepan, melt the jam over medium heat, stirring frequently. Remove from the heat and stir in the softened gelatin. Stir in the salt and the blueberries. Stir gently with a wooden spatula so that all the blueberries are coated, then pour the blueberry mixture into the prepared crust.

Refrigerate for an hour or more to chill well. Spread the Mascarpone Cream over the top and serve cold.

Makes one 9-inch pie / 8 wonderful servings

NOTE: I adore the Mascarpone Cream more than anything, but you could use 2 cups of sour cream sweetened with ¼ cup of packed dark brown sugar, or 1 cup of heavy cream, whipped and sweetened with 2 tablespoons of sugar.

Mascarpone Cream

This is my absolute favorite topping for fruit in the whole world. Food writer and teacher Michele Scicolone introduced me to the joy of mascarpone and honey. Stirring the honey into the mascarpone lightens it and makes blending it with the whipped cream easier. Chilling the cream, bowl, and beaters helps fat stick together around the air bubbles to hold the whipped cream firm.

What This Recipe Shows

Cheese triggers umami flavor receptors.

Cheese and heavy cream carry both fat-soluble and water-soluble flavors.

½ cup mascarpone cheese
2 tablespoons honey
1 cup heavy or whipping cream

In a small bowl, whisk together the mascarpone and honey. Place a medium bowl and beaters in the freezer for 5 minutes. In the cold bowl using the cold beaters, whip the cream to medium-firm peaks. Fold the mascarpone mixture into the whipped cream. Chill until ready to serve. Serve cold.

Makes about 2½ cups

FRUIT JELLY

Fruit jelly is an elusive substance. Ideally, it is a quivering solid of transparent, beautiful color, formed when sweetened fruit juice is immobilized—trapped in spaces when huge pectin molecules link together.

If you have ever made jelly, the directions sound easy enough. For simple classic jelly, you crush some fruit in a saucepan, add only enough water to barely show under the fruit, and cook until the fruit is soft and begins to lose its color. Strain the contents of the pot through a jelly bag (unbleached muslin). Place 4 cups of the strained juice into a large, flat-bottomed stainless-steel or enamel pot. Simmer for about 5 minutes. Stir in ¾ cup to 1 cup of sugar. Boil until it reaches 220° to 222°F. (Without a thermometer, boil for 10 minutes, then spoon up a small amount of jelly, let it cool slightly, then let it drop from the side of the spoon back into the pot. At first, the drip is light and syrupy; then it gets thick enough to fall in two large drops from the edge of the spoon. Finally, it gets thick enough to drop in a single big dollop.) When the jelly reaches the single-drop stage, pour it into sterilized jars and cover with melted paraffin. When the paraffin hardens, put the lids on. Easy enough—however, sometimes it works, and sometimes it doesn't.

First, you have to have a sufficient amount of pectin. You don't have a chance unless you use a high-pectin fruit and one that is acidic like crab apples, tart apples, sour blackberries, red currants, gooseberries, sour plums, lemons, or cranberries. Sweet apples, prune plums, and some varieties of oranges and quince have plenty of pectin but not enough acid to make a jelly that will set. Fruit will work best if it is not quite ripe— still acidic.

But what if you want to make jelly with apricots, strawberries, or pomegranates? They are acidic, but don't have enough good-quality pectin. And then there are peaches and pears and nearly any overripe fruit, which has neither pectin nor acidity. How can you make jelly with these?

You have two choices. You can add a high-pectin acidic fruit to the mix, or you can add commercial pectin, which is extracted from the pith of citrus fruit or apple cores, and a little of an acidic ingredient.

Acidity is important because pectin molecules are charged, and they repel each other just like the same ends of magnets do. Acids neutralize the charge so that the pectin molecules no longer repel each other and can join. This is why fruits that are not ripe, that are still acidic, form the best jellies. Or you can add a little lemon juice or vinegar when you initially boil the fruit.

An even better idea is to add a few lemon slices, peel and all, when you initially boil the fruit. The pith (the white part of the peel) is very high in pectin and is used as a source of commercial pectin. And the yellow lemon zest will impart wonderful flavor, providing that much-needed acid.

But pectin molecules would rather join with water than with each other. This is where the sugar comes in—it grabs the water so that it's not available for the pectin. So, we now have three necessities—acidity, enough pectin, and enough sugar. With natural pectin from boiling the fruit, a sufficient amount of sugar is needed. Don't think that you can get a more healthful jelly by reducing the sugar—it simply won't gel.

There are commercial pectins (low-ester pectins) that have undergone reactions to change their structure so they will join and make jellies with little or no sugar. There are also fast-setting gels and slow-setting gels available.

In the technical literature, I often see calcium mentioned—calcium ions increase gel strength or ensure gelling. The only easy kitchen source of calcium that I can think of is molasses. You might try ½ teaspoon of molasses in your next batch of jelly.

You can see that a good jelly is a work of art—you have to have just the right balance of pectin, acid, and sugar. I always took for granted the cupboard full of sparkling colored jams and jellies that my grandmother made, but I really have respect for it now. My grandmother must have been a genius to get all those different fruits to gel.

Color Changes in Red Fruits and Vegetables

The three types of red compounds in fruits and vegetables are:

1) Betalains—deep red like beets. Betalains are water-soluble and will stain other foods.
2) Anthocyanins—blue-reds like red cabbage, berries, red grapes, apples, and peaches. Anthocyanins are very water-soluble, and fruits or vegetables containing them can fade. They also have to be acidic to stay red.
3) Carotenoid compounds—orange-reds like tomatoes and red bell peppers, and orange and yellows like carrots, pumpkins, sweet potatoes, rutabagas, and squash. These compounds are fat-soluble, and fruits and vegetables containing them retain their color well unless severely overcooked.

Betalains

Beets turn from red to deep violet when strongly acidic (pH below 4).

Beets turn yellow when strongly alkaline (pH above 10).

Anthocyanins

Red cabbage turns blue. Anthocyanins must be acidic to stay red. When some acids evaporate in cooking, they can turn blue. Add lemon juice or vinegar and the anthocyanins, and therefore the cabbage, will turn back to bright red.

Cherries in muffins may have a blue circle around them. An acidic ingredient (sour cream, buttermilk, or lemon

111

juice) substituted or added to the muffin batter may help.

Walnuts (which have this same compound just under the skin) may discolor dishes blue. Roasting walnuts will prevent discoloration.

Red grapes in a sauce lose their color upon standing. Fruit with anthocyanins are soluble in water. Their color will fade upon standing in a sauce or dressing. Wait until serving to stir grapes or berries into a sauce or dressing. Use reddish ingredients in sauces or dressings to enhance color.

Red cabbage or fruit or vegetable juice turns green. Anthocyanins turn blue when alkaline and flavones or flavonols turn yellow. If a fruit or vegetable has both, the resulting color will be green when alkaline.

Red fruits or vegetables turn green, slate gray, or blue. Metals like iron or aluminum from cookware can react with anthocyanins when alkaline to produce green, slate gray, or blue compounds.

Other Color Changes

Potatoes or onions turn yellow or brown. Flavonoid compounds turn yellow or brown when alkaline and also in the presence of metals like aluminum or iron. Add a little vinegar or cream of tartar to the cooking water to prevent discoloration.

Garlic in vinegar turns blue. When garlic is very fresh, harmless proteins in some varieties or possibly contributed by soil conditions turn blue when acidic.

Carotenoids

We have known that these orange foods were good for us. Our mothers told us to eat our carrots—they would make our eyes sharper. They do, indeed, contain carotenoid compounds, the precursors of vitamin A, which is essential for normal growth and development, immune system function, and vision. The addition of vitamin A precursors to some strains of rice has dramatically cut infant mortality and blindness in Asian countries where diets were very low in vitamin A.

A number of fruits and vegetables, such as carrots, spinach, peaches, apricots, and sweet potatoes, contain beta-carotene. Other vitamin A precursor carotenoids include alpha-carotene (found in carrots, pumpkin, and red and yellow peppers) and cryptoxanthin (from oranges, tangerines, peaches, nectarines, and papayas). Lycopene, the carotenoid that gives tomatoes their red color, is particularly effective at quenching the destructive potential of singlet oxygen. Singlet oxygen is a highly reactive form.

Animals (cows, sheep, chickens, and we humans, too) are totally dependent on plants to make food for us. The green chlorophyll compounds of plants are photosynthesis centers that (with the energy from sunlight) join carbon dioxide and water together to make glucose. Plants then pack this glucose together and store it in the form of starch. It is this starch that provides food for all animals.

I had always connected green chlorophyll only with photosynthesis. I had no idea that orange, red, and yellow carotenoids had anything to do with it. Actually, carotenoids are essential for the survival and productivity of all photosynthetic organisms. Carotenoids perform two major functions in photosynthesis. They are accessory light-harvesting pigments (in the red, yellow, and orange range), extending the range of wavelengths over which light can drive photosynthesis, and they protect the chlorophyll pigments from the harmful photodestructive reaction, which occurs in the presence of oxygen.

These red, yellow, and orange carotenoids are in plant leaves all the time. We don't know that they are there in the spring and summer because the green chlorophyll hides them. But in the fall, when the temperature becomes cold enough to kill the chlorophyll, we see the bright yellow, orange, and red colors of the leaves. These carotenoids were there all the time—just hidden by the green chlorophyll.

Carotenoids dissolve in fat, not water, and are relatively stable. Unless they are badly overcooked, they do not lose their color. Red bell peppers seem to stay red forever. Carotenoids are so stable that they are used as natural colorants for other foods. Extracts of annatto, alfalfa, carrots, paprika, and tomatoes are all used as natural coloring agents.

Many chemical compounds have the same basic composition but differ only in the detailed way their atoms are arranged. Carotenoids change their structure with prolonged overcooking and this is why their color eventually changes. As they go from the intensely colored trans structure to the paler cis structure, there is a corresponding change in the color of the vegetable. Cis and trans structures are two different ways that the same atoms are joined together. The same number and type of atoms are in the carotenoid, but in the cis configuration two functional groups are on the same side. In the trans configuration the functional groups are on opposite sides.

You may have noticed that badly overcooked yellow squash becomes pale and washed-out looking. There is an exception to this. Rutabaga go from the paler cis structure to the more intense trans structure and become a deeper orange when cooked. Carrots and pumpkins have such large amounts of carotene that they usually retain their color even when overcooked.

Here are two recipes that feature carotenoids—Shirley's Great Pumpkin, a deep-orange roasted pumpkin filled with herbed barley, beans, and chickpeas, and Golden Tomato Bake, an easy, delicious, year-round (with good canned tomatoes) side dish.

SHIRLEY'S GREAT PUMPKIN

Even a huge roasted-to-perfection turkey takes a back seat to this magnificent browned pumpkin filled with the most intriguing aromas, cooked with herbed barley, beans, and onions. My daughter, Terry, and I are fond of Annemarie Colbin's recipes in both *The Book of Whole Meals* and *The Natural Gourmet*. Terry prepares a stuffed pumpkin similar to Annemarie's. I tried to preserve the drama of the dish in my version. A small to medium pumpkin is ideal for this dish. You can also use small sugar pumpkins, which are very sweet and have thicker flesh. Simply use two of them instead of one medium jack-o'-lantern type of pumpkin. If a pumpkin is not available, use another large squash, such as spaghetti squash, turban squash, etc.

Juices from the pumpkin add sweet complex flavors to the grain and bean filling. Note that sesame oil should not be heated to high temperatures, and ordinarily is used in small quantities as an added flavoring. The temperature is kept low here to avoid damage to the oil.

> ### What This Recipe Shows
>
> Orange carotenoid fruits and vegetables retain their color and nutrients even when cooked for a long time at a high temperature.
>
> Sesame oil and chile oil carry fat-soluble flavors.

1 fresh pumpkin, washed well, about 10 inches in diameter
2 garlic cloves, minced
2 large onions, chopped
¼ cup toasted sesame oil
3 cups quick-cooking barley
2 (14.5-ounce) cans chicken stock
3 cups water
1 (16-ounce) can chickpeas, drained and rinsed
3 (16-ounce) cans navy beans, drained and rinsed
1 tablespoon dried oregano
2 teaspoons dried basil
2 teaspoons dried rosemary
½ cup orange marmalade
¼ cup packed light brown sugar
½ cup chopped fresh parsley
¼ cup soy sauce
1 teaspoon fine sea salt
½ teaspoon ground pepper
2 tablespoons Chinese hot chile oil
Large green leaves, for garnish

Arrange a shelf in the lower center of the oven and preheat the oven to 400°F.

Cut the top from the pumpkin slightly lower than you would if carving a jack-o'-lantern and set the top aside. Scoop out and discard the seeds. Set the pumpkin aside.

In a large skillet, cook the garlic and onions in the sesame oil over low to medium heat until the onions are just translucent, not brown. In a large saucepan, combine the barley, stock, and water and cook at a low simmer for 10 minutes.

In a large bowl, stir together the onion mixture, barley, chickpeas, navy beans, oregano, basil, rosemary, orange marmalade, brown sugar, parsley, soy sauce, salt, pepper, and chile oil. Spoon the mixture into the pumpkin and fit the top back in place. Place on a small pizza pan and bake in the oven for 1 hour. The pumpkin should be well browned.

Serve the pumpkin surrounded by large green leaves (clean magnolia leaves for appearance, not to eat). Remove the top and lean it against the side of the pumpkin. Cut around the top edge and serve a small piece of the pumpkin with the filling.

Makes 12 servings

GOLDEN TOMATO BAKE

In this modern version of my grandmother's stewed tomatoes, a crunchy, buttered-crumb topping covers the tomatoes, which are accented with fresh basil and lemon zest. Jane Brock, an outstanding creative cook in Jackson, Mississippi, introduced me to the simple crusty topping, which I like much better than stirring in the crumbs.

Tomatoes retain their color fairly well in baking, but not their texture, making them good for casseroles. Mixing the butter with some of the crumbs produces a more even distribution of the butter than simply pouring it on top.

What This Recipe Shows

Sugar preserves the tomato's texture.

Pepper and intense-flavored lemon zest add flavor.

Butter carries fat-soluble flavors.

---

4 (14½-ounce) cans diced tomatoes

4 ripe medium tomatoes, peeled, seeded, and chopped
    (if using fresh tomatoes, save a long strip of peel
    from one) or 2 (14½-ounce) cans DelMonte tomato
    wedges, drained

1½ teaspoons finely ground sea salt, plus more if needed

1 teaspoon ground pepper

Zest of 1 lemon

9 fresh basil leaves, thinly sliced lengthwise

2 cups fine bread crumbs

⅓ cup packed light brown sugar

6 tablespoons (¾ stick) butter, softened

2 pretty sprigs fresh basil, for garnish

Preheat the oven to 350°F.

In a large bowl, stir together the diced tomatoes and fresh tomatoes. Add the salt, pepper, lemon zest, and basil leaves and stir together well. Taste and add more salt if necessary. Spoon the tomato mixture into a 9 by 6 by 3-inch baking casserole. Sprinkle evenly with 1½ cups of the bread crumbs.

In a medium bowl, mix together the light brown sugar, remaining ½ cup bread crumbs, and the butter. Sprinkle the butter-crumb mixture evenly over the tomato mixture. Bake for 20 to 25 minutes, until the tomatoes are bubbling and the crust is lightly browned. Garnish with a tomato rose (made by coiling a long piece of tomato peel). Arrange the fresh basil sprigs with the rose. Serve hot, at room temperature, or even cold.

Makes about 12 servings

THE BEST TOMATOES!

Even if you are not a gardener, you may have neighbors or relatives who bestow generous amounts of fresh vegetables upon you. If you are lucky, you may have real, honest-to-goodness tomatoes—deep red, ripe, and sweet. They do not even resemble the hard, pale, tasteless "tomatoes" in the grocery store.

If you are the gardener, you can carefully pick the tomato variety. Read the descriptions in the seed catalog and select a variety that has the characteristics that you want.

Ripe Tomatoes

Fried green tomatoes are a treasured Southern dish, but many flavor changes take place in tomatoes as they ripen, and truly ripe ones are wonderful. Vegetables, like zucchini, may be at their best picked small. But with tomatoes, if you can, leave them on the vine as long as possible.

Technically, a tomato is a fruit (the seed-bearing ovary of a plant). It is all-important for the plant to take care of its seeds. As tomatoes grow, they are a protective green to hide among the leaves. When the seeds are fully developed and ready to sow, the tomato has a problem. If all its seeds fall clumped together right under the plant, there will be only a limited amount of nutrients for them, so only a portion of the seeds will get the food and sunlight they need to prosper.

So, the tomato seeks the help of animals (humans included) to spread its seeds. If the tomato becomes desirable both in appearance and taste, animals will grab it, carry it away, eat it, and take the seeds to other places. The tomato goes from a hidden green to a luscious, stand-out red or yellow.

Major taste changes take place in the tomatoes as they ripen. They become less acidic and much sweeter. Big starch molecules break down into sugars to make the tomatoes more appealing.

There are also changes in glutamate, a compound that stimulates your umami taste receptors. In a ripening tomato, glutamate goes from 10 mg per 100 ml of juice to 100 mg per 100 ml of juice. This reflects the dramatic change from a cardboard-tasting unripe tomato to the absolutely delicious flavors in a truly ripe tomato.

Caring for Tomatoes

Now that we have this treasure—ripe, truly delicious tomatoes—how do we care for and serve them? First, do not refrigerate them—a major flavor compound in tomatoes, (Z)-3-hexenal, is destroyed by chilling.

Remember the complex influences of salt and sugar on flavor described in chapter one. You do not need to taste the salt or the sugar itself, but you can use just enough to take advantage of their magic and bring out the flavors in a dish.

The amount of salt and sugar in the recipe for Ripe Tomatoes and Mozzarella is small, ¼ teaspoon each, but flavor-wise, this can make a big difference.

Ripe cherry or grape tomatoes or chopped larger tomatoes can be a crowning glory for many dishes. I love to lightly brown garlic slices in olive oil and toss them with spaghetti. This can be a company dish when topped with coarsely chopped ripe tomatoes and cut slivers of fresh basil leaves. My friend Sara Risch's dish that follows is similar, but a little more elegant.

RIPE TOMATOES AND MOZZARELLA

Delicious ripe tomato slices are alternated with slices of mild white mozzarella and topped with a drizzle of olive oil and strips of bright green fresh basil. A light sprinkle of salt and sugar brings out the tomato's rich flavors. My mother always insisted on peeling the tomatoes, but you don't have to.

2 large ripe tomatoes, peeled and cut into ½-inch-thick
   slices

¼ teaspoon fine sea salt

¼ teaspoon sugar

6 ounces mozzarella cheese, cut into slices less than
    ¼ inch thick

¼ cup your favorite olive oil (James Plagniol, Filippo
    Berio, or a Moroccan olive oil are my favorites)

6 fresh basil leaves, cut at an angle into long strips

Sprinkle the tomato slices with the salt and then with the sugar.

Arrange the tomato and mozzarella slices alternating on a platter.

Drizzle with the olive oil and garnish with the basil.

Makes 4 servings

ORZO WITH TOMATOES
AND GORGONZOLA

Dr. Sara Risch is an internationally renowned flavor chemist, and a good friend of mine. We have done many programs together for the American Chemical Society. With red tomatoes and bright green fresh basil slivers, Sara makes this easy, beautiful, and incredibly flavorful side dish. It can be expanded to a main course by adding raw seafood (shrimp or even salmon) 5 to 10 minutes (or enough time to thoroughly cook the seafood) before it is done, or by adding chopped cooked Italian sausage to the orzo a few minutes before it is done. You could also add broccoli florets or another vegetable about five minutes before the orzo is done.

You can prepare the orzo ahead and even cut the tomatoes and toss them with olive oil. Then, when you are ready to serve, stir salt and pepper into the tomatoes, reheat the orzo, stir in the Gorgonzola and butter, assemble, and serve. The onions become sweeter as they are cooked. Granular bouillon is used for its more intense flavor. The tomatoes are tossed with a tiny bit of sugar to preserve their shape and for flavor.

What This Recipe Shows

Chicken bouillon contributes more intense flavor than stock.

Gorgonzola and butter carry fat-soluble and water-soluble flavors.

---

1 large onion, coarsely chopped
6 tablespoons olive oil, divided
3 garlic cloves, minced
1 pint cherry or grape tomatoes
1 teaspoon sugar
Salt (preferably finely ground sea salt) and ground black
    pepper
About 3 cups water
3 to 4 tablespoons granular chicken bouillon
1⅓ cups orzo

2 ounces Gorgonzola cheese, labeled pasteurized (if
    you don't like Gorgonzola, another pasteurized blue
    cheese may be substituted)
3 tablespoons butter
10 fresh basil leaves, cut into long slivers

In a heavy pot, cook the onion in 3 tablespoons of the oil over low heat until they are very soft, about 20 minutes. Stir in the garlic and cook for about 5 minutes more.

While the onion is cooking, slice the tomatoes in half and, in a large bowl, toss with the sugar first, and then with the remaining 3 tablespoons of oil. Add the salt and pepper to taste.

When the onion is very soft, add the water and chicken bouillon. Bring to a full boil, then add the orzo. Cook over medium heat, stirring steadily, until the orzo is done, about 20 minutes, depending on the size of the orzo. Mash the Gorgonzola and butter together and add to the hot orzo. Toss the Gorgonzola mixture with the orzo to melt and coat. Spoon onto a warm serving platter. Pour the tomatoes on top and garnish with the basil.

*Makes 4 servings as a main course or
6 servings as a side dish*

NOTE: Pasteurized Gorgonzola is recommended because it, among some other soft cheeses, can contain *Listeria monocytogenes*, which can cause very serious illness for at-risk groups, including the young and old and those with health conditions.

CHILES — WHAT'S HOT AND WHAT'S NOT

I always thought that the seeds and veins in chiles were where the heat was. Not exactly. Dr. Paul Bosland of the Chile Pepper Institute explains that pepper pods are fruits, the seed-bearing ovaries of a plant.

Pools of all five capsaicinoid compounds are produced by glands located on the surface of the placenta. The placenta (on the inside of the pepper) is the white pithy part attached to the top of the pepper that grows downward that the seeds are attached to. In lower heat peppers, the capsaicin glands (yellow in color), the hottest part of the pepper, are only on the surface between the placenta and seeds. So if you don't want a spicy jalapeño (lower heat pepper), carefully scrape the light-colored part, bringing the seeds with it, out of the pepper.

However, on higher heat peppers the capsaicin glands are actually all over the inside walls (the glands are oblong to round sacs in a mottled or spotted pattern) of the pepper, as well as on the surface of the placenta. Every knife cut releases some capsaicin from these peppers, splattering the hot capsaicin throughout the inside of the pod. So every cut matters on these hot peppers.

Every Cut Matters

Handling the superhot peppers requires caution: wear gloves and don't touch your face or eyes. Every cut into these peppers releases capsaicin. Small pieces of the wall of these peppers may contain a great deal of spice. The steam from cooking can also contain heat.

Five Compounds

It was originally thought that capsaicin was one compound, but the fiery crystalline extract from peppers contains five compounds that scientists refer to as capsaicinoids: capsaicin (69 percent), dihydrocapsaicin (22 percent), nordihydrocapsaicin (7 percent), homocapsaicin (1 percent), and homodihydrocapsaicin (1 percent). Dr. John Powers and Anna Krajewska of the University of Georgia studied professional taste-testers' responses to the separate compounds. Nordihydrocapsaicin was described as the "least irritating" and "fruity, sweet, and spicy," and homodihydrocapsaicin as "very irritating" with a "numbing burn" in the throat.

How to Cool the Heat

Water is no help. The "fiery" capsaicinoid compounds are colorless, odorless, tasteless, powerful alkaloids that are not soluble in water but are very soluble in fat and alcohol. Would something fatty or alcoholic relieve the agony?

Fat and alcohol are more soothing than water, but milk will give you more relief than anything. In 1989, John Riley, editor of the journal *Solanaceae*, tested various remedies to remove the burn from chile peppers. Participants chewed a slice of a serrano chile for 1 minute, then various remedies were applied and the amount of time until the burning sensation subsided was recorded.

John Riley's Burn Remedy Test	
Remedy	Minutes Until Relief
Rinse the mouth with water	11
Rinse the mouth with 1 tablespoon olive oil	10
Drink ½ cup heavy fruit syrup	10
Rinse the mouth with 1 tablespoon glycerin	8
Drink ½ cup milk, rinsing well	7

Robert Henkin of the Taste and Smell Clinic in Washington, DC, says that casein, a phosphoprotein found in milk, acts as a detergent and strips the capsaicin from the nerve receptor binding sites in the mouth.

In a 1990 study at the University of California–Davis, Christina Wu Nasrawi and Rose Marie Pangborn reported that a 10 percent sucrose solution at 20°C (68°F) was just as effective as milk at 5°C (41°F). This may explain why some think that sugar can reduce the heat in a dish that is excessively hot. Another solution is to add a little vinegar. I like to simmer jalapeño slices in ½ cup vinegar, 1 cup sugar, and 2 cups water to reduce their heat and produce a mellow taste. The cooking liquid is a great flavoring agent, too.

NOT ALL FRUITS AND VEGETABLES ARE GOOD FOR YOU

We tend to think that everything "fresh and natural" is good for us, but when it comes to survival, Mother Nature means business. Many things that are "fresh and natural" are deadly poisonous.

Plants can't run from predators like animals can. So, to save themselves or their young, plants resort to chemical warfare. If you have ever cried while chopping onions, you have experienced this. When you cut into (attack) an onion, chemicals that have been locked away in one part of the onion's cells now come in contact with chemicals isolated in another section and together they produce a gas that irritates animals' (humans included) eyes. This can be a successful way to drive predators away.

The seeds of many plants are poisonous to ensure the safety of the next generation. Apricot pits, peach pits, and apple seeds, to name a few, are full of cyanide. Fortunately, they are rarely eaten.

Though we may not think of them as such, beans are seeds, too, and some contain "protective" compounds. Lima beans, like peach pits and apple seeds, contain cyanide. Some varieties have such a high cyanide content that they are not allowed to be grown commercially in the US. When limas are cooked, this cyanide converts to a gas and escapes harmlessly into the air. You should not, however, eat raw lima beans. Beans, such as soybeans, contain enzyme inhibitors that prevent protein digestion. They cause chemical changes in the lining of the intestines that make it impossible for nutrients to be absorbed. These enzymes are killed by heat, so beans are harmless when cooked, but should not be eaten raw. Prolonged eating of raw beans can result in death.

Many other plants that are used as foods can be toxic if not prepared properly. Cassava (yuca), a plant that is a major food source in many parts of the world, contains cyanide, but traditional preparation—chopping or mashing and allowing the cassava to stand—allows enzymes in the cassava to react and convert the cyanide to harmless compounds. As long as cassava is prepared in this traditional way, it is a nutritious food source. However, when modern chefs roast cassava in the skin like a baked potato, the cyanide remains.

All potatoes contain harmless, small amounts (5 mg per 100 g) of solanine, a poison common to members of the nightshade family. The eyes of potatoes and the area under the green chlorophyll resulting when potatoes are left in the light can increase solanine content up to 200 mg per 100 g, a significantly more dangerous amount. If there are small green spots or eyes only, and no green on the skin, cut them out and all around them, otherwise throw the potato out. Do not serve to children and never eat a bitter-tasting potato. Select carefully to avoid green potatoes and store in a cool, dark place with good air circulation.

Jerusalem artichokes (sunchokes) do not contain toxins; however, they do contain large sugars known as oligosaccharides. These are the compounds in beans that produce flatulence. Native Americans sliced Jerusalem artichokes thinly, boiled them, discarded the cooking liquid (which contained a lot of the sugars, extracted from the tubers), and enjoyed them very much. Settlers, unfamiliar with this New World food, roasted them whole in the fire, which did not remove these sugars, and they unfortunately suffered the results!

Throughout the southeastern United States, we have a large weed called poke salad or pokeweed (*Phytolacca americana*) that has been enjoyed by locals for many years. It is always prepared by boiling young green leaves from the plant, discarding the cooking water, boiling and discarding the water again, then boiling the leaves a final time before eating them. The soluble toxic compounds are removed by boiling, and the greens are then safe to eat and nutritious.

Parsley contains two known toxins, myristicin and apiole.

129

Normally, parsley is used in small amounts or as a garnish. Dishes containing large amounts of parsley like tabbouleh should not be eaten on a regular basis.

Parts of some plants are deadly and should never be eaten. A healthy adult can die in hours after eating rhubarb leaves, which contain anthraquinone glycosides and can cause organ failure. You may have noticed that fresh rhubarb sold in grocery stores always has the leaves removed.

Fruits can contain poisons, too. A chemical similar to the irritant compound in poison sumac is located just under the skin of mangoes. Some people are more sensitive to this than others and can experience mango rash, an itchy red rash on any skin exposed to this part of the mango.

We all know that some mushrooms are deadly poisonous, but some are powerful hallucinogens. Different types of hallucinogenic mushrooms found in Mexico have been used in religious ceremonies. For safety, only eat wild mushrooms gathered and properly identified by an expert.

Nutmeg also contains powerful hallucinogenic compounds. A sprinkle in your eggnog is fine, but if you eat two or three whole shaved nutmegs, you may find yourself in outer space.

Our food supply is very safe. Plants have been bred for generations to improve size, taste, and nutrient content and to minimize their toxins. Cooking and traditional methods of preparation remove toxins. It is, however, good to have a healthy respect for plants. Just because it is "natural" does not mean it is good for you.

CHAPTER FOUR

BEANS, TUBERS, AND GRAINS

BEANS, BEANS, BEANS

Legumes are a truly ancient food. It is thought that lentils were cultivated as far back as 7000 BC. They are an excellent source of protein and fiber and, combined with grains, have been an important food for many cultures.

Nutrition

Generally speaking, legumes have about half the protein of meat and twice the protein of cereals (grains) per serving. Protein content varies from about 34 percent in soybeans to about 20 percent in lima beans. Legumes have higher-quality protein than cereals, and they are a better source of some of the essential amino acids like lysine, isoleucine, leucine, phenylalanine, threonine, and valine. However, legumes are a poor source of the amino acids methionine and cystine, which are available in cereals. So, legume-cereal combinations like beans and rice complement each other to provide all the essential amino acids.

With the exception of soybeans and peanuts, most

legumes are very low in fat. Their high soluble and insoluble fiber content can help reduce cholesterol levels and stabilize blood sugar levels, making you feel "full" longer. In addition, legumes contain vitamins (B1, B2, B3, B6, and E) and minerals (calcium, potassium, and iron).

Dried beans contain lectins, which are toxic. Raw soybeans contain a growth inhibitor, and most beans, including soybeans, contain a trypsin inhibitor. Fortunately, cooking destroys these compounds, which inhibit nutrient absorption in our bodies.

Lima beans actually contain cyanide. Varieties grown in the US have been bred for very low cyanide content, but some types grown in Asia have quite high cyanide contents. Again, fortunately, cooking dissipates this cyanide as a gas making the beans harmless.

Beans contain large sugars called oligosaccharides, which pass untouched through the upper intestines and become a feast for bacteria in the lower intestines. Unfortunately, these bacteria produce quantities of flatulence as they devour the sugars. Of course, the amount of gas will vary greatly from individual to individual according to the bacteria in their intestines. And different varieties of beans like navy and great northern beans seem to be more gas-producing than others, even though they do not have higher oligosaccharide contents. So, it is quite possible that other compounds in legumes contribute to gas, too.

These sugars are water-soluble, and rinsing dried beans several times before cooking is a help in reducing gas. Plus, dried beans cook faster if they are soaked before cooking. The water initially enters the bean through the hilum (or scar), where the bean was attached to the stem in the pod. After some water has been absorbed by the bean, it starts to soak through the bean's seed coat. Beans with thinner coatings soften faster.

The temperature of the soaking water also matters. The warmer the water, the faster it is absorbed. This has led to the "quick-soak" procedure. To do this, rinse the beans several times and discard any "floaters." Put the beans in a large pot and cover with 4 cups of water for each cup of beans. Bring the water to a boil, then reduce the heat to keep the water at a low simmer for 2 to 10 minutes. Turn off the heat, cover, and allow to stand for 1 hour.

Beans can also be soaked overnight in room-temperature water. If your kitchen is very warm, you may need to refrigerate the beans (in their soaking water) after 3 or 4 hours to avoid sprouting.

The beans and water can be heated to a boil in the microwave and quick-soaked for about 1½ hours.

Storage and Preparation

Beans should be stored in an airtight container in a cool place. One of the most common problems with dried beans is the "hard to cook" phenomenon. You can soak some beans overnight and then cook them all day and they remain hard. One cause of this is improper storage. If beans have been stored under high temperature (around 100°F) and high humidity (80 percent) conditions, they can be almost impossible to cook. Soaking in salt water before cooking can eliminate this problem. If you have difficult-to-cook beans, soak your next batch in salt water (1 tablespoon of salt per gallon of water) for 2 hours.

Cooking not only gets rid of protease inhibitors—enzymes that prevent us from digesting proteins—but it increases the availability of nutrients and the palatability of the beans.

One objection to beans, especially soybeans, is their beany taste. Adding salt to the cooking water from the beginning is a major flavor enhancer. You may have been told not to salt beans early in cooking or they will not soften. This is simply not true. There are things that prevent softening, but salt is not one of them.

Naturally hard water containing calcium and/or magnesium prevents softening. Adding ingredients containing calcium or sugar also slows or prevents the softening of beans. Heat normally causes the insoluble pectin substances (the "glue" between the cells) to convert to water-soluble pectins, which dissolve. The cells then separate and the beans soften. However, both calcium and sugar hinder this conversion to pectin. Thus, adding either calcium or sugar to a food will help keep its firm texture.

When cooking dried beans, you should use 3 to 4 cups of water for each cup of beans. You can count on getting 2 to 2½ cups cooked beans for each cup of dried beans. Bring the water to a boil, then turn down the heat so the water is just below a simmer and cook until the beans are tender.

Many recipes suggest 1 tablespoon fat for each cup of beans. I like to use country ham, ham hocks, bay leaves, thyme, and sea salt when cooking most beans. The table below gives approximate cooking times, but always taste and make sure the beans are tender instead of relying on exact times.

Cooking Times for Beans			
	Soaking	Water	Cooking Time
Adzuki	Unsoaked	4 cups	1½ hours
	Soaked	4 cups	1 hour
Black (turtle)	Soaked	4 cups	1½ hours

	Soaking	Water	Cooking Time
Black-eyed peas	Soaked	3 cups	1 hour
Chickpeas	Soaked	4 cups	2 to 3 hours
Great northern	Soaked	3 cups	1½ hours
Kidney	Soaked	3 cups	1 hour
Lentils	Unsoaked	3 cups	1½ hours
	Soaked	3 cups	45 minutes
Lima	Soaked	3 cups	1 hour
Navy	Soaked	3 cups	1 hour
Pinto	Soaked	3 cups	2 to 2½ hours
Soybeans	Soaked	4 cups	3 to 4 hours
Split peas	Soaked	3 cups	45 minutes

Approximate Times with Different Cooking Methods		
Pressure cooker—(use about 2½ cups water)		
Soaked	20 to 30 minutes	
Unsoaked	40 to 50 minutes	
Slow cooker		
Soaking and cooking	12 hours on Low	
Microwave		
Soaked	50 minutes	

THE LENTIL EXPERIMENT

I couldn't wait to get home from the conference on molecular gastronomy in Erice, Sicily. We had covered everything from the change in the texture of a baba au rhum (rum-soaked cake) caused by the addition of the eggs at different times to tobacco in food. Leslie Forbes, a former BBC reporter, a great food writer (author of the book *A Taste of Tuscany: Classic Recipes from the Heart of Italy* and others), and also a mystery novelist (her novel *Bombay Ice* was in all the airport newsstands), was at the meeting. She wanted to know why housewives in India added a little minced ginger and a few fresh spinach leaves to their lentils to "make them creamy."

Now, there is a single enzyme in ginger that attacks both muscle fiber and gelatin. This is why ginger is a tenderizer and why it prevents gelatin from setting. It was reasonable to think that ginger could have some effect on the proteins in the lentils. I couldn't wait to get home and try it.

What the spinach was doing, I didn't know. Possibly some oxalic acid in the spinach reacts with and removes any calcium in the water. Calcium, like sugar, allows fruits and vegetables to remain firmer when cooking because it prevents the pectic glue between the cells from changing to water-soluble pectins.

What I needed to do was cook lentils plain, cook the same amount with ginger, the same amount with spinach, and finally the same amount with both ginger and spinach, as the Indian cooks do. I could then compare them to see what each ingredient was doing to the lentils.

The day I got home—jet-lagged as I was—I made two batches of lentils in identical pots. I put equal amounts of lentils and water in each, then to one I added 2 tablespoons minced fresh ginger (a great excess). I soaked and cooked the two pots of lentils at the same heat level for the same length of time. The lentils cooked with the ginger absorbed more water. They were between ¾ inch and 1 inch higher in the pot, and they were definitely more tender.

The ginger lentils were more tender, but not "creamy." Now I was really anxious to see if the addition of spinach changed the situation.

An extract from spinach is more effective than other plant extracts in preventing the loss of elasticity in fish gels. In investigating this, researchers found a multicatalytic protease complex that has at least three types of activities. What all this means is that spinach has enzymes that can do different things to proteins.

I shredded a few fresh spinach leaves and stirred them into a strong mixture of clear gelatin to see if the spinach would prevent the gelatin from setting. But, alas, the gelatin set firmly. So, whatever these enzymes were doing, they were not attacking gelatin.

I put the same amount of lentils and water in a pot as before. This time, I added a more reasonable amount of minced ginger—a scant tablespoon—and ten small fresh spinach leaves. I soaked and cooked the lentils in the same manner as I had the other two pots.

To the eye, the lentils with both spinach and ginger did not look different, but wow, was there a taste-texture difference! Somehow, in the mouth, you get a perception of smoothness. Whatever it is, there is something in spinach that changes the mouthfeel of the lentils—they were definitely smoother. Try it for yourself. Or next time you are cooking any kind of dried beans or lentils, throw in a little minced ginger and a few fresh spinach leaves. And I love a little ham in my lentils. Go with your favorite recipe, or try mine, below.

CREAMY LENTILS

Adding minced fresh ginger and fresh spinach is a recipe tip from Indian housewives for creamy lentils that truly works.

What This Recipe Shows

Minced ginger contains an enzyme that breaks down both protein and collagen to produce tenderer lentils.

Fresh spinach leaves contribute to creamier lentils.

---

10 small fresh spinach leaves
1 cup dried lentils, well rinsed and cleaned of any debris
2 teaspoons minced fresh ginger
4 cups chicken stock or water
1 large onion, finely chopped
2 tablespoons vegetable oil
4 ounces cooked ham (such as smoked picnic ham
    pieces), finely chopped

On the bottom of a medium (2½- to 3-quart) saucepan, place the spinach leaves and pile the lentils and ginger on top to keep the spinach from floating. Gently pour the stock down the side of the pot. Allow the lentils to soak for 45 minutes to 1 hour.

Place the saucepan over low heat. While the lentils are heating, in a small pan, sauté the onion in the oil for 5 minutes, then add the ham and sauté for 2 minutes. Add the onion and ham to the lentils. After 10 minutes on low, turn the heat up to medium and bring the liquid to a simmer. Simmer for 20 to 30 minutes, until the lentils are tender. Serve hot. Leftovers can be refrigerated and reheated.

Makes 4 servings

POTATOES

Mashed potatoes can really soothe the soul. Wonderfully warm, soft, creamy—you can feel a mouthful go down, warming you all the way.

It's not as easy as you might think to prepare potatoes that make you feel that good. But with a little insight into the different potato varieties and preparation techniques suited to the starchy tuber, you can make dishes that consistently satisfy.

Potatoes come in all sizes, shapes, and textures, from round little new potatoes with a dense, waxy, moist texture to large, high-starch Russet Burbank potatoes with a light, dry, almost fluffy texture. You can use any potato in any job, but you get a better dish using the right potato.

The big russets make magnificent, fluffy baked potatoes or excellent nongreasy french fries. They are also good for mashed potatoes. The dense, waxy, little new potatoes are ideal for boiling and make great potato salad. They tend to have a sweeter taste since they are young and small (their sugars haven't converted to starch yet). There are also the flavorful yellow-fleshed potatoes like Yukon Gold, Agria, and Golden Wonder. Their wonderful buttery taste makes these my favorite for mashed potatoes. Many love them for crisp french fries.

Potato Storage

Ideally, potatoes should be stored in a cool, dark place with good air circulation. When potatoes are exposed to light, they develop a green color, indicating the presence of solanine, a very toxic poison. If there are small green spots or eyes only, and no green on the skin, cut them out and all around them, otherwise throw the potato out. Do not serve to children and never eat a bitter-tasting potato. Select carefully to avoid green potatoes and store in a cool, dark place with good air circulation.

Ideal storage is cool, not cold. I once had a call from a cruise ship executive chef who was distressed over their baked potatoes. Even though they bought the best high-starch russet potatoes, their baked potatoes did not have the desirable fluffy texture. Cruise ships have refrigerated storage rooms and unrefrigerated rooms down in the hull of the ship, which get extremely hot. The potatoes were refrigerated because they would spoil right away in the extreme heat.

Unfortunately, when potatoes are refrigerated, their starches convert to sugars, which wreck the fluffy, starchy texture. The good news is that this is a reversible reaction. If you keep the potatoes warm for a day, their sugars convert back to starch. I recommended that the ship's cooks move a day's worth of potatoes to a hot room each day. Using potatoes that had been hot for twenty-four hours, their baked potatoes were fluffy again.

Refrigeration can be a disaster if you're planning to make french fries, too, causing them to get too dark before they are done.

Why Some Potatoes Don't Cook

I have had many calls about potatoes that wouldn't cook. Pat and Betty, the Reynolds Kitchens girls, were developing whole meals (a meat, a starch, and a vegetable) in foil packets. They had one in which the potatoes remained rock hard after more than an hour of cooking. They thought the potato pieces were too big, but when they got them down to the size of rice and they were still rock hard, they called me.

To minimize the number of ingredients, instead of using salt, pepper, basil, etc., Pat and Betty used a tablespoon or two of a salad dressing. The dressing in this dish was a very acidic vinaigrette. Starch granules won't swell and soften (i.e., the potatoes won't cook) in acidic conditions. They switched dressings, and the potatoes were perfect.

This can also be a problem with potatoes that are cooked in sour cream. You can precook the potatoes in water or milk until they are soft and then bake them in sour cream.

How to Minimize Discoloration

Cooked potatoes can discolor, turning dark on one end (called stem-end blackening). This is caused by iron compounds that come from growing in rich soil. You can minimize this by adding a small amount of lemon juice or vinegar to the cooking water.

Keeping Mashed Potatoes Hot

You wait until just before serving to prepare mashed potatoes so that they will be hot. You mash them in the hot pot, but despite your efforts, the potatoes are never really hot when you serve them. The problem is that you are beating room-temperature air into them. The secret is to mash the potatoes ahead. Totally prepare them: add the cream, butter, and salt, and mash. Spoon them into a heatproof casserole and heat them in the oven for 40 minutes at 325°F. Taste and add seasoning if needed. If you have done them an hour or so ahead, you can leave them on the counter. If you prepare (all except the baking) them a day ahead, cover and refrigerate them.

Before serving, cover the casserole tightly with foil and bake at 325°F for 40 minutes. Now, these potatoes are HOT all the way through, and they will stay hot. Even the scoop on your plate stays hot!

MASHING POTATOES

Potatoes can become gluey if you break a lot of the starch granules in mashing. If you mash potatoes in a food processor, you really shear the starch granules and will get a gluey mess—wallpaper paste.

You can mash with an old-fashioned potato masher or with a large fork, or mix with a mixer just enough to get the lumps out—an absolute minimum. Or cook them until they are very soft and press them through a ricer. Or, you can cook the potatoes ahead and cool them completely and then mash them. When you thoroughly cool them, the starch crystallizes and is no longer water-soluble and won't become gluey.

Great Fries

Frying potatoes—how complicated can that be? You take a potato, cut it into strips, cook 'em in oil until they're brown, take 'em out, and drain. Nothing to it. Well, I don't know. There are other factors like, "What kind of potato?"

The high-starch potatoes like Russet Burbanks (Idahos) absorb less fat, cook in less time, produce light, crisp fries that do not easily become soggy, and are the preferred frying potato of many cooks. The Burbanks have larger starch granules than other varieties. When these potatoes are cooked, their large starch granules absorb all the water between the cells, causing the cells to separate and producing the dry, fluffy texture that we love in baked potatoes. In frying, this produces a crisp, never soggy or limp fry.

However, this is not the only potato that can be used for frying. In *The Man Who Ate Everything*, Jeffery Steingarten points out that there may even be cultural preferences for different potatoes. Americans like the dry, granular interior texture of Russet Burbanks while Europeans prefer the moister, smoother texture of slightly lower-starch potatoes regardless of their increased fat absorption.

Most supermarkets offer some of these slightly lower-starch potatoes—not the small, "waxy" red potatoes, which are excellent for boiling and potato salad, but all-purpose eastern varieties like Katahdin, Maine, and Kennebec, to name a few.

Yukon Golds, buttery-tasting yellow potatoes, are even a little lower in starch but are still used for frying because of their great taste.

Fries can be cut any size, but for them to cook through at the same time, they need to be uniform. The classic french fry has a ⅜-inch square cross section and is about 3 inches long.

Technically speaking, the smaller and thinner the food, the faster it will be done, and the greater its surface area. Greater surface area means more surface for the oil to be absorbed and faster moisture loss.

Rinsed, Not Rinsed, Chill or Ice Water Soak, Wet or Dry?

Early-harvested potatoes have a higher starch content and a lot of starch on the surface from slicing. It is the natural reducing sugars and proteins in potatoes that brown. So, rinsing off this starchy coating can enhance browning.

For very crisp fries, the Idaho Potato Commission recommends chilling the potatoes for up to 2 hours before cooking.

Drying the surface of the fries is a great help in several ways. First, the evaporating water cools the cooking fat and requires a longer time for it to come back up to cooking temperature. This will eventually require a longer cooking time and mean more fat absorption.

Water also reacts with the cooking fat, forming contaminates that lower the smoke point of the fat.

Meanwhile, as the starch granules get hot, they absorb moisture and swell. With perfect conditions, the starch on the surface absorbs water from the interior and swells to seal the surface, while the interior starch absorbs the rest of the water, producing a crisp, dry surface and a dry, non-soggy interior.

Water on the surface can mess things up. It will take longer for the surface starch to absorb all this water and get a dry surface that seals.

A chef or caterer who has a busy day ahead may cut potatoes for french fries, place them in a large container of ice water, and store them in the walk-in refrigerator overnight. The next day, when these potatoes are fried, they get very dark and look done but are raw in the center. These potatoes fried perfectly the day before. What happened?

When potatoes (and a number of other starchy vegetables) stay chilled for a period of time, some of the starch breaks down into sugar. Now these higher-sugar-content potatoes brown much faster. The sugar and protein content, along with the acidity, determine how fast a food will brown. If left at room temperature for a day or so, the sugars will join back together to form starch. If you have stored whole potatoes at a cool temperature, you may want to leave them at room temperature a day before frying them.

Cooks can use this little bit of science to make better low-fat oven fries. One of the problems with making fake french fries by roasting potato strips in the oven is that they do not get very brown. If you soak cut potatoes in ice water in the refrigerator overnight (maybe even add a little sugar to the water), steam them for a few minutes to partially cook them, then toss them in something alkaline (less acidic) like slightly old egg whites (lightly beaten) and sprinkle them generously with herbs, cayenne, salt, pepper, and a small amount of Parmesan, these potatoes will brown nicely in a hot oven. Be generous with the seasonings. Remember, one of the great problems with low-fat cookery is lack of flavor.

How to Fry

Chefs have all kinds of preferences when it comes to fats for frying potatoes—everything from duck and goose fat to beef fat. Many of us remember how wonderful McDonald's fries were when they were cooked in beef tallow.

Highly saturated fats like coconut oil are the superior frying fats. They have a high smoke point, are not absorbed as easily as other fats, are stable, and produce crisp fried products with an excellent shelf life. But from a health standpoint, they elevate serum cholesterol.

Most vegetable oils—peanut, corn, canola, cottonseed, and safflower—have moderately high smoke points. Tastewise, peanut and corn oils, with their slightly nutty overtones, may be preferred over soy and canola oils, which have flavor notes closer to a bean.

There is nothing wrong with a blend—mostly fresh peanut oil with a little fresh bacon drippings for flavor. In an article in *Cook's Illustrated*, Fred Thomas used a blend like this, and I think the taste is good.

Commercial frying fats are designed for reuse and have additives for safety, but fats for home use do not. For home frying, the absolute most important factor for both safety and quality is to use fresh oil. Any noncommercial fat that has been used at high temperatures, even just once, can have a very low smoke point, and I consider this dangerous.

For outstanding fries, they should be prefried at a low temperature to cook them through, then fried briefly at a high temperature to brown and crisp them. I use the same oil for the initial cooking and final frying, but I dispose of it after the higher temperature use.

Experts vary in recommended times and temperatures for each frying. The Idaho Potato Commission recommends precooking with the frying fat at 350°F until the fries just begin to color, then draining. You can hold the fries in a single layer on a baking sheet at room temperature or even refrigerate them, covered, overnight. When you are ready to serve, fry them again with the fat at 375°F until lightly brown and crisp. Drain them on paper towels, season with salt, and serve immediately.

Some chefs prefer a longer, lower-temperature precook—anywhere from 265°F to 325°F.

Not all chefs insist on the double-fry procedure. The famous French chef Joël Robuchon was said to fry his potatoes by starting cold, dry potato strips in cold peanut oil in a deep (at least four-inch-high sides), heavy pan placed over high heat and simply frying the potatoes until they were a deep golden brown (never allowing the oil to get over 370°F), then draining, salting, and eating them.

Chef Robuchon, I think you've got something here!

SWEET POTATO SECRETS

Have you ever had a sweet potato that would not cook—that stayed rock hard after hours in the oven? What causes this? Sara Moulton of *Sara's Weeknight Meals* asked this question. In spite of her frantic schedule, she cooks daily for her family and frequently serves baked sweet potatoes because of their great nutrient content and her children's love of them. I didn't know the answer, but I knew that Dr. Rob Shewfelt at the University of Georgia would.

Amazingly, this is a chill injury. Sweet potatoes are a tropical plant and, like bananas, they are injured by cold temperatures—below about 55°F. Bananas that are chilled never ripen; they just turn brown and rot. Chilled sweet potatoes suffer what is termed "hard core condition." They have a bitter taste and stay hard as a rock no matter how long you cook them.

To avoid sweet potatoes that will not cook, never refrigerate them and never buy sweet potatoes in a refrigerated produce section.

There are many varieties of sweet potato, but the two major categories are the moist, sweet, orange-fleshed varieties with dark orange or copper skin and the dry, yellow-fleshed varieties with light skin. For the sweet variety, select firm potatoes with smooth, deep-copper-colored skin, with no bruises, sprouts, decay, or off odors.

Sweet potatoes (*Ipomoea batatas*) are edible storage roots, not tubers like potatoes. They are a member of the morning glory family and have a lovely vine with flowers that look like morning glories. North Carolina's Jewel variety and Louisiana's Beauregards (both with sweet, moist, deep-orange flesh) make up about half of the US sweet potato crop.

True yams are a different species in the genus *Dioscorea*. They need long, warm growing seasons and are raised only in tropical and subtropical regions. They vary greatly in size, with some tubers growing up to seven feet in length (some weighing a hundred pounds). They have scaly rough skin that ranges in color from off-white to brown.

If sweet potatoes and yams are totally different, why do we call sweet potatoes "yams"? Before 1930, all sweet potato varieties in the US had been the dry, yellow-fleshed kind, not the sweet types. Then, a new, deep-orange, really sweet variety was introduced and the promoters wanted everyone to realize these were different from the dry, pale-fleshed sweet potatoes people were accustomed to, so they marketed the new sweet potatoes as "yams." Common usage has made the term "yam" acceptable for all sweet potatoes. Officially, there have been attempts to distinguish between the two, such as the US Department of Agriculture requiring the moist-fleshed, orange-colored sweet potatoes labeled as "yams" to also be accompanied by the label "sweet potato," but this does not always happen.

Cooking

Sweet potatoes are a nutrition gold mine and can be prepared in many ways—baked, boiled, broiled, fried, microwaved, or even grated raw and added to slaw or salads.

A popular appetizer at OK Cafe, a busy Atlanta restaurant, is a plate of very thin-sliced deep-fried sweet potato chips with a blue cheese dip. Because of their high sugar content, sweet potatoes brown fast when frying, so you must watch them carefully.

A baked sweet potato is wonderful and truly easy to cook. I love to serve them baked, split open, and covered with butter, brown sugar, and, for real luxury, some chopped roasted pecans.

In *On Food and Cooking*, Harold McGee explains that baking is a great way to cook sweet potatoes because they actually get sweeter. Sweet potatoes contain an enzyme that converts their starch to the sugar maltose during cooking. The enzyme becomes active around 135°F, when the tightly packed starch granules absorb moisture and swell. These enzymes remain active until they are killed at 170°F. Baking, which is a slower cooking method than boiling or microwaving, allows these enzymes a longer time to make a sweet potato sweeter. Many recipes instruct you to bake sweet potatoes at 400°F to 450°F, but you will get a sweeter potato by baking them at a lower temperature—maybe around 300°F.

Sweet potato casseroles run the gamut from savory layers of sweet potatoes, onions, herbs, parsnips, etc., to the standard cooked, sweetened, and pureed sweet potatoes with melted marshmallow topping. The following Old-Fashioned Sweet Potato Pudding recipe is delicious, and a refreshing difference from today's casseroles.

Yellow and dark orange sweet potatoes can be used interchangeably in recipes, but it is better not to mix the two types in a single dish, because they have different cooking times. The yellow variety takes longer to cook than the orange.

Like many other fruits and vegetable, sweet potatoes contain phenolic compounds that will combine with oxygen and darken when cut surfaces are exposed to the air. Vitamin C prevents this reaction, so you can put cut sweet potatoes in a bowl with orange juice to preserve their color.

Sweet potatoes are virtual powerhouses of nutrition—packed with beta-carotene (vitamin A), high in vitamin C, and an important source of vitamin B6, iron, potassium, and fiber. Sweet potatoes seem to be one of the current save-us-from-everything foods. There is ongoing research on nutrients in sweet potatoes for memory enhancement, diabetes control, recovery from respiratory infections, and reduction of the risk of heart disease and cancer.

OLD-FASHIONED
SWEET POTATO PUDDING

This is my grandmother's recipe and was a traditional way of preparing sweet potatoes in her mother's time. One of my students, who prepares this every Christmas, took a dish to a nursing home. She said that tears rolled down the cheeks of one of the seniors as she ate these sweet potatoes. The elderly lady said, "I haven't had sweet potatoes like this since I was a girl."

The sweet potatoes are grated raw and baked as a custard with ginger as the predominant flavoring.

What This Recipe Shows

Stirring after partially baking prevents the outer edges from overcooking before the center is done.

Cornmeal serves as a starch preventing the eggs from curdling.

Nonstick spray
1 pound sweet potatoes (2 large or 3 small), peeled and
    cut into chunks
½ cup packed dark brown sugar
½ cup packed light brown sugar
¾ teaspoon salt
2 teaspoons ground ginger
3 tablespoons cornmeal
1 large egg
2 large egg yolks
1 cup heavy or whipping cream
1 tablespoon vanilla extract

Preheat the oven to 325°F. Spray a 9 by 6 by 3-inch casserole with nonstick spray.

Working in several batches, put the sweet potatoes in a food processor and pulse until finely chopped into pieces the size of large grains of rice (or you can grate the potatoes by hand). In a large bowl, mix together the sweet potatoes, dark and light brown sugars, salt, ginger, and cornmeal. Stir the egg, egg yolks, cream, and vanilla into the sweet potato mixture.

Pour the mixture into the prepared casserole and bake for 15 minutes. Stir from the outside to the middle (see Note), then bake for 10 minutes more and stir again. Bake for about 15 minutes more, until lightly browned and just set. Serve hot or at room temperature. The sugar can be halved and milk used in place of cream and still give a delicious casserole.

Makes 8 servings

NOTE: The typical problems of a baked casserole are that the edges tend to overcook and get dry before the center is done. My grandmother minimized the problem by stirring twice during cooking before the custard set firmly.

RICE

When a Japanese chef prepares sushi, he reaches for cooked short-grain rice. He easily shapes the sticky rice into mounds on which to lay pieces of fish, or packs it neatly into sushi rolls. When an American chef makes rice pilaf, she begins with raw long-grain rice. Once cooked, the individual grains remain pleasantly separate, soft but not sticky. Switch the two kinds of rice, and you'd get pilaf that clumps together and sushi rolls that fall apart.

Before you cook rice, it helps to understand its specific characteristics. The most important factor is the composition of the rice's starch.

What Is Starch?

Starch is made through photosynthesis. Using energy from the sun, plants combine carbon dioxide and water into simple glucose, or sugar molecules. These glucose molecules either link into long chains to make the kind of starch called amylose, or they link into many short, branched chains to make amylopectin. Both kinds of starch are packed tightly together to form granules.

All plants contain both types of starch, but with different ratios of amylose and amylopectin. Long-grain rice has more amylose; short-grain rice has more amylopectin.

Heat Makes Rice Exude Starch, Some Kinds More Than Others

When you heat starch in a liquid, the molecules of both the starch and the liquid move faster, and water seeps into the starch granules. As the temperature rises, more water gets in and the granules swell. Somewhere near the boiling point of water, some of the swollen granules pop, and starch rushes out into the liquid. (When you're making a sauce or a gravy, this is when it thickens.)

In short-grain rice, the starch granules (which are mostly amylopectin) swell and pop at around 160°F to 170°F. High-amylose long-grain rice doesn't finish swelling until about 200°F, meaning that in the same cooking time, it gives off less starch than short-grain rice does, which means that long-grain rice stays separate. Medium-grain rice is between the two in its starch characteristics.

Creamy with a "bite" is the hallmark of great risotto.

Cooking Arborio rice in a little liquid makes the starch granules on the outside of the rice grains pop, while the center granules only swell. The popped granules exude starch, making the dish creamy, while the unpopped granules keep the centers of the grains firm.

Choosing the Right Rice

All rice is grouped into three categories: long-grain (the length is at least three times the width), medium-grain (the length is about two times the width), and short-grain (the length is less than two times the width). Long-grain and short-grain rices are not interchangeable; medium-grain rice is similar to short-grain.

Type of rice	Long-grain	Medium-grain	Short-grain
Description	High in amylose. Cooks into fluffy, separate grains.	Lower in amylose than long-grain. Can be used in place of short-grain.	High in amylopectin and low in amylose. Cooks soft and sticky.
Popular types	Carolina, basmati, jasmine	Arborio, black japonica	Sushi, Spanish, pearl
Good for	Rice pilafs, rice salads (tossed with dressing while warm), white rice side dishes	Rice salads, rice puddings, risottos	Sushi, paellas, stir-fries, rice puddings

Type of rice	Long-grain	Medium-grain	Short-grain
Problems	Cooled rice becomes rock hard and stays hard unless reheated and served warm.	Can clump as it cools.	Can become mushy if cooked with too much liquid.

Cooking with Long-Grain Rice

As cooked long-grain rice cools, those long amylose molecules move more slowly and bond tightly to each other. Because long-grain rice has more amylose than short-grain, it can become rock hard.

Not only does cooked long-grain rice harden, but once cooled, much of its starch becomes insoluble, and won't soften even if you add liquid. If you reheat the rice, the bonds of amylose will break, and the rice will become soft again. But in dishes where the rice is cooked and chilled but not reheated—as in rice salads—amylose crystallization can be disastrous. You end up with pebblelike rice that isn't even softened by a vinaigrette.

To avoid this problem, mix the rice with moist ingredients (such as vinaigrette, in the case of rice salad) while the rice is still hot. The additional liquid soaks in to keep the amylose molecules separate so they can't bond and harden. Alternatively, you can use medium-grain rice, which has less amylose and will not harden as it cools.

While you can use cooled and hardened rice in rice pudding, you'll want to eat it while it's still warm. Once cooled, the amylose will make the rice hard once again.

Long-grain rice can contribute to another problem in rice pudding—the settling of the rice. If it's not cooked long enough, or if it has been cooked and cooled, it doesn't exude starch to aid in thickening. If the custard doesn't thicken fast enough to suspend the rice, the rice falls to the bottom of the dish.

For this reason, many rice pudding recipes call for short- or medium-grain rice, because it exudes starch at a lower temperature. Many long-grain rice pudding recipes either initially overcook the rice so that it's very starchy, or they call for enough eggs and a high cooking temperature to help set the pudding quickly.

CHAPTER FIVE

PERFECT SAUCES

Sauces are the crowning glory to a meal. They add moisture to dry foods, add flavor, enhance appearance, and can improve your meals overall. Here is how to make smooth, creamy, flavorful sauces.

PUREES

Purees can be used to thicken a sauce, or can themselves be a sauce.

Pureed vegetables can be beautiful, but taste bland, because they may have little or no fat to carry flavor. To remedy this, add some fat and/or alcohol (sherry, brandy) to carry flavors, or add flavorful components like lemon or orange zest or ginger. Marcella Hazan's famous tomato sauce has 5 tablespoons of butter and an onion to 2 cups of tomatoes.

Purees made with nuts like walnuts, almonds, or hazelnuts and fine bread crumbs, thinned with stock and reduced, make wonderful sauces. Claudia Roden's Circassian Chicken recipe in *A Book of Middle Eastern Food* is a classic example of a sauce thickened with 1 cup pureed walnuts and 1 cup bread crumbs in 2 cups stock, reduced until thick enough to coat the back of a spoon. It has been called "the most comforting chicken dish ever."

STARCH-THICKENED SAUCES

Sauces containing starches, like cornstarch, flour, potato starch, arrowroot powder, tapioca starch, rice starch, etc., are a heartier accompaniment to a meal.

Starches are granules, composed of layer after layer of glucose polymers (glucose polymers are single units of glucose or other sugars joined together to form larges molecules). The starch granules are insoluble in a cold liquid, but as the liquid warms, it seeps into the granules and causes them to swell. Starchy foods, like rice, potatoes, and pasta, soften (cook) as the granules swell. As the liquid is heated and more and more seeps into the granule, it swells to many times its original size and finally pops. In making a sauce or gravy, this is when starch rushes out into the sauce and thickens it.

When you are making a sauce, you can't see the starches swelling. You may get impatient and think, "This is not thickening enough" and add a little more cornstarch in cold water. Then, all at once, you reach that magic temperature where the starch granules pop, and you have absolute glue! Some starches do not completely thicken until right around the boiling point. The secret to working with these sauces is to wait until they reach a gentle boil before deciding if you need to add more starch.

All starches absorb a large weight of water, but the granules are different sizes and swell to different sizes. You can see from the following chart that different amounts of different starches are required to thicken sauces. Cornstarch swells to about twenty times its original volume before it pops, while potato starch can swell to one hundred times its original size before popping.

Since these large potato starch granules are full of moisture, pastry chef and author Bruce Healy substitutes a small portion of potato starch for flour (about 10 percent substitution) in his pound cake to make a moister cake. The potato starch loosens the extremely tight structure of the cake. Visually, the structure is still dense but the taste is lighter.

Each starch granule contains two kinds of glucose polymers—amylose (a long, straight, bar-shaped molecule) and amylopectin (a little branched molecule with points sticking out in many directions like a multipointed star). These starches behave differently when cooked. When amylose reaches the temperature that the granule pops and the starch molecules rush out into the sauce, both the long, bulky amylose molecules and the puffed, empty granules contribute to the thickening. When the starch cools, amylose molecules bond to each other to make a firm, slightly opaque gel. Amylopectin molecules and the empty granules contribute to thickening, but the little amylopectin molecules do not join together to form a solid gel.

Amylose makes sauces and gravies that may be clear when hot but cloudy (slightly opaque) when cooled and very thick— thick enough to cut with a knife—when cold. Sauces or gravies made with a high-amylose starch freeze badly, forming a dry, spongy mess in a runny puddle. Amylopectin makes sauces that are crystal clear hot or cold, but never get firm enough to cut with a knife. High-amylopectin sauces freeze and thaw beautifully.

Ordinary grain starches like wheat and corn are relatively high in amylose, containing about 26 percent, while root starches like arrowroot and tapioca (from the cassava plant) contain less, about 17 to 21 percent. Potatoes are a tuber, not a true root, and potato starch falls somewhere in between, with about 23 percent amylose. Some types of "waxy" cereal starches (for example, waxy cornstarch) are very high in amylopectin (99 percent). These high-amylopectin starches and modified starches (man-made starches that are altered to have specific characteristics) are the mainstay of the frozen food industry.

Sometimes you will need one kind of starch and sometimes another. If you are making a coconut cream pie, you definitely need it firm enough to cut, but it doesn't matter if it is opaque. On the other hand, for a cherry pie, you want a clear thickener. It would be a shame to have a cloudy covering on bright red cherries.

It is possible to have your cake and eat it, too. In cherry pie, you can use primarily tapioca starch, but add just a little cornstarch to make it thicker—not enough to give a cloudy appearance.

Home cooks have a number of starches available to them. Cornstarch and flour are usually in the baking section, and arrowroot powder is sold in the spice aisle. Most large markets have potato starch, but it is not shelved with the cornstarch; it is often found with the Jewish cooking ingredients, next to matzo meal. The best place to buy starches is an Asian market. It has tapioca starch (a powder, not pearls like you'd use in tapioca pudding), rice starch, arrowroot powder, and many others at a fraction of the supermarket price. For example, a medium bag of arrowroot powder may cost as little as $1.50 at an Asian market, compared to $5.00 for a few tablespoons in a jar at the supermarket.

Grain and Root Starches Compared	
Grain Starches	**Root and Waxy Starches**
High amylose—up to 28 percent	High amylopectin—up to 99 percent
Transparent at gelation temperature; slightly opaque when cool.	Transparent during gelation; transparent and glossy when cool.
Thickens at gelation temperature; becomes even thicker as it cools and sets into a firm gel that can be molded or sliced.	Is thickest at gelation; thins some as it cools.
Thickens at just below the boiling point of water; can be held at this temperature without damage.	Thickens at a lower temperature (167°F); may thin if overheated.
Withstands moderate mechanical action (stirring) without thinning gelation while hot; once set into a solid gel, stirring will thin it.	Sauce may thin dramatically if stirred hard after it reaches temperature.
Reheats without thinning.	Thins when reheated.
Becomes spongy and leaks watery fluid when frozen and thawed.	Freezes and thaws well without change.

How Much Starch to Use

In general, the amounts of flour per cup of liquid to use for a sauce are:

Thin sauce: 1 tablespoon flour per 1 cup liquid
Medium-thickness sauce: 2 tablespoons flour per 1 cup liquid
Thick sauce: 3 tablespoons flour per 1 cup liquid

Other starches are completely different.

Starch Needed to Thicken 1 Cup of Liquid	
Starch	Amount Needed for Medium-Thickness Sauce
Grain Starches	
Cornstarch	1 tablespoon + 1 teaspoon
Flour	2 tablespoons
Rice starch	1 tablespoon + ½ teaspoon
Root and Tuber Starches	
Arrowroot powder	1 tablespoon + 1 teaspoon
Potato starch	2¼ teaspoons
Tapioca starch (Asian market)	1 tablespoon + 1 teaspoon
Quick tapioca pudding starch (supermarket)	1 tablespoon + ¼ teaspoon

Techniques for Starch-Thickened Sauces

All these methods below (roux, beurre manié, and slurry) permit the starch to be released granule by granule to avoid lumps. They involve mixing the starch with fat, which disperses the starch granule by granule when it melts, or mixing the starch with water.

> **Roux:** Melt fat and stir in flour. The darker the roux, the less its thickening ability. Heating starches to high temperatures damages the granules and they can no longer swell and thicken as they normally do. Some chefs make a dark roux for flavor, but then add a light roux for thickening. Then add your liquid (milk, cream, or stock) slowly, stirring constantly to form the sauce from the roux. A cream sauce thickened with a roux is called a béchamel or balsamella.
>
> **Slurry:** Stir starch into cold water to disperse.
>
> **Beurre manié:** In a cup or small bowl, off the heat, blend together a starch (normally flour) and butter by smushing them together to form a paste. The paste is called a beurre manié. To make sauces with a beurre manié, heat a small part of the liquid (milk, cream, or stock over medium heat). Whisk the beurre manié into the warm liquid with constant stirring. Add more liquid with constant stirring to get the thickness desired.

The most common sauce is a cream sauce made with milk and/or cream, thickened by one of the above methods.

Using the above methods, it is also possible to make sauces with low-fat dairy products (which have a lot of protein and not much fat to prevent the proteins from coagulating when they are heated—i.e., curdling). It is vital to use starch to prevent these sauces from curdling.

REDUCTION SAUCES

A reduction sauce can be anything from a rich, complex veal demi-glace to a quick, delicious pan sauce that you make from the bits left over after you sauté a couple of steaks. Indeed, many fine sauces owe their marvelous complex taste and silky body to this basic technique: classic stock-based sauces such as chasseur and Bordelaise, red and white wine sauces, and many cream sauces. Even sauces that get their body through means other than reducing, like a béchamel (which is thickened with a roux), improve in flavor when simmered a bit to concentrate and transform their ingredients.

Reducing, which happens through simmering or boiling, removes water by evaporation, and therefore concentrates and intensifies flavors, but less water is only one of the reasons reduced liquids taste good. Some acids and other strong-tasting compounds have low boiling points and are actually boiled off, enhancing the flavor of the remaining liquid by their removal. Not only are some unpleasant-tasting compounds removed, some potential problem ingredients are removed, too. For example, when you reduce wine, tannins and other compounds that might cause any cream in the sauce to curdle are boiled off.

Even more changes take place as your liquid simmers away. The high heat speeds up chemical reactions, and some compounds in the sauce break apart while others join together, creating new compounds that have totally different flavors.

During the reduction, the liquid boils and some spatters on the pan just above the surface level of the sauce. As the sauce reduces, some particles of dried sauce are left on the pan. This dried sauce gets quite hot since it isn't protected by liquid. The sauce contains both proteins and sugars from the meat, wine, and stock. At this higher heat, complex browning reactions (called the Maillard reaction, see the section "Browning" in Chapter One: Flavor) take place with the protein and sugars. Many of the same wonderful sweet compounds that form when sugar is caramelized are produced. Then, when you stir and splash the sauce back on these dried compounds, many are redissolved into the sauce.

The flavors of your final sauce will of course be determined by how much you reduce the ingredients, but also by when each ingredient is reduced. A sauce made by reducing wine, adding stock and reducing it, then adding cream and reducing that will taste much different than one made by combining wine, stock, and cream and reducing them all together.

Some chefs even use multiple reductions of the same ingredient to get complex layers of flavor. For example, a classic French jus (an intensely flavored, light-bodied sauce) is made from repeated reductions of a small amount of stock added to a mirepoix and browned bones. You add the stock, cook it almost dry (taking care not to let it burn), add more stock, cook it almost dry again, and repeat the process until the liquid is very flavorful. Each time you cook the pan almost dry, you allow the mirepoix and bones and glazy liquid to deepen in flavor. By adding more stock, you dissolve the wonderful brown sweet compounds that were created. This sauce will taste entirely different (and much better, I think) than a sauce made with the same amount of stock added to the mirepoix and bones and just reduced slowly in one go.

Here's one way to make a quick and delicious reduction sauce: Start by deglazing the skillet after you've sautéd seasoned pieces of meat (beef, pork, veal, lamb) in a little fat. When the meat is cooked, transfer it to a plate and keep it warm. Pour off the fat, add red or white wine (or other flavorful alcohol, such as cognac or calvados) to the skillet, and simmer the liquid, scraping the pan to loosen any stuck-on meat particles, until there are just a few tablespoons of syrupy liquid left. Next add a little stock and reduce again until the liquid is intensely flavored and slightly syrupy. Finally, add a little cream or crème fraîche and reduce until the sauce thickens slightly. You have only to taste, add seasonings as needed, and spoon the wonderful hot sauce over the meat. In a medium to large heavy skillet over high heat, the whole process takes only a few minutes.

Tips for Successful Reduction Sauces

- If you're using wine in a sauce, be sure to use a decent-quality one, something that you'd drink with the meal you're making, if possible.
- Don't make a reduction sauce with regular canned stock: it's generally quite salty to begin with and will be too highly salted when reduced. Homemade stock is best, if you have it, or use a low-sodium prepared stock.
- If you plan to finish the sauce with cream, be sure that any wine or other alcohol has been sufficiently cooked off before adding the cream, to prevent curdling.
- Once a reduction sauce is finished, don't try holding it over low heat, because it will continue to reduce slowly. Instead, take it off the heat and reheat gently just before serving. This is especially important if the sauce was

finished with cream or butter: the emulsion that was formed between the liquids and the fat in the cream or butter can break if not enough liquid remains to go between the droplets of fat. Free fat will form at the edges and on top of the sauce. If this happens, you can usually reverse it by whisking in a little water or stock to restore an adequate liquid-to-fat balance.

EMULSIONS

An emulsion is a mixture of two liquids that ordinarily do not mix, like oil and water. Fine droplets of one of the liquids are dispersed in the other liquid.

An emulsion can be oil droplets dispersed in water like mayonnaise and hollandaise, or water droplets dispersed in oil or fat like butter or beurre blanc. The amount of one liquid or the other does not determine the type of emulsion. It is the emulsifier. Emulsifiers lower the surface tension of one of the liquids more than the other and make it "juicy" so it can run between the droplets of the other liquid.

To get a stable emulsion, one liquid must be broken into tiny drops and the drops must be kept apart somehow. If they run into each other, they will join together to form bigger and bigger drops and finally separate out of the emulsion. The other liquid must be "juicy" and run between the drops. Breaking one of the liquids into tiny drops is easily done with a blender, food processor, or whisk. Emulsifiers handle the other two tasks. They make one of the liquids "juicy" so it can run between the droplets, and they coat each droplet of the other liquid to prevent their joining.

Natural emulsifiers in egg yolks hold fat and water

together in many foods, including sauces like hollandaise, béarnaise, and mayonnaise and in batters for cakes, cream puffs, etc. Emulsions affect the texture of foods in two ways: Emulsifiers in an egg yolk can coat liquids with fats to create smooth, creamy textures in everything from custards to chocolate truffles. Emulsifiers also thicken. In mayonnaise, an egg yolk (the emulsifier) helps pack an entire cup of tiny oil droplets into about 2 tablespoons of liquid (vinegar or lemon juice), producing the thick texture of mayonnaise. An egg yolk (pasteurized) or butter whisked into a sauce after it is removed from the heat binds fats and liquids for a slight thickening and improved texture.

Three Basic Requirements for Stable Emulsions

1) **An emulsifier.** Chemical emulsifiers are natural or man-made molecules that have one end that dissolves in oil and another end that dissolves in water. Egg yolks contain phospholipids, lecithin, and many other molecules that are emulsifiers. Emulsifiers reduce the surface tension of one of the liquids, making it "juicy" so it can run between drops of the other liquid, and coat the droplets themselves with molecules, which stick out and keep the droplets themselves from running together.

2) **Mechanical action to break one of the liquids into tiny droplets.** In making mayonnaise, a blender, food processor, or whisk breaks oil into droplets as it is slowly drizzled into the other liquid and an emulsifier. Drizzle the oil in slowly at first because the oil droplets are not yet packed and have room to easily scoot out of the way of the blade.

3) **Enough of the liquid that goes between the drops.** Even
   if the droplets of the first liquid are coated with an emulsifier and bounce off each other, if there is not enough
   liquid to go between those drops, they will be forced
   together and will not form an emulsion. This can be a
   problem with mayonnaise, hollandaise, or any emulsion.
   Most whole-egg mayonnaise recipes work well because
   they contain water from the egg white, but some egg
   yolk–only mayonnaise recipes are tricky. The recipes
   that fail frequently do not have enough vinegar, lemon
   juice, or other watery liquid to go between the drops.

Problems with Emulsions

- **Mayonnaise recipe "does not work."** Mayonnaise
  needs at least a tablespoon of water-type liquid to hold
  the emulsion. With egg yolk–only mayonnaise recipes,
  if there is not enough lemon juice or vinegar (water-
  type liquid), the emulsion will not hold.
- **Mayonnaise is thin.** Whisk in the oil **very** slowly at first.
- **Mayonnaise made with olive oil breaks.** Harold McGee
  points out that extra-virgin olive oil contains mono-
  glycerides that can cause emulsions to break. Switch to
  pure olive oil for a mayonnaise that will hold. There are
  different kinds of olive oils. For example, extra virgin,
  pure olive oil, and plain olive oil, which can be a mixture of olive oils from all over the world. My preference
  is pure olive oil.
- **Hollandaise or béarnaise sauce turns into scrambled
  eggs and melted butter.** The sauce is too hot. You get
  scrambled eggs at 180°F.

169

- **Hollandaise or béarnaise sauce starts to separate.** The sauce might be getting too hot or running low on water-type liquid. Remove it from the heat and whisk in some cold, water-type liquid (water, lemon juice, vinegar).
- **Hollandaise or béarnaise sauce is too thin.** If egg yolks and lemon juice are ice cold and melted butter is barely melted, the sauce will not get hot enough for the egg yolks to thicken it. Pour the sauce into a warm container in which butter was melted and whisk. Heat carefully over low heat, with constant whisking, until it begins to thicken.
- **Beurre blanc or beurre rouge (butter sauces) separate.** These sauces break at 136°F, which is not very hot. Your beurre blanc can be saved by cooling and whisking. They also separate when refrigerated. To re-form a refrigerated beurre blanc, heat ¼ cup heavy cream to reduce, then whisk in the refrigerated sauce, adding it a few spoonfuls at a time.

CHAPTER SIX

ON FREEZING

Some foods freeze well and others don't. So, which do and which don't? Certain foods, like baked goods, can be frozen as is, while others require special treatment. What are the secrets of freezing and thawing for a quality product?

The rate of freezing has a major influence on food quality. Rapid freezing minimizes the size of the ice crystals and damage to the cells. Large crystals can rupture cell walls and produce soft or mushy textures. Commercial products use rapid-freeze methods like direct immersion in a freezing medium, indirect contact with the refrigerant, or a blast freezer. Properly operating home freezers are set at about 0°F and can sharp freeze, which is in the range of 24°F to −20°F. Foods frozen between 25°F and 31°F are said to slow freeze, and will have larger crystals and a poorer texture.

Place food to be frozen on a lower shelf of the freezer, which is usually several degrees colder than the upper shelves. Once the food is frozen solid, it can be placed on another shelf.

Another very important item for freezing foods is nonpermeable wrap. Wrap for frozen food must be both moisture- and vapor-proof. Many plastic wraps, waxed paper, and even foil have tiny holes through which moisture and oxygen can pass. Be sure to use only plastic bags, nonpermeable plastic

171

wrap (like Saran), or containers labeled "freezer" and squeeze out as much air as you can before sealing them. There should be as little air space around the food as possible.

Here are some of the best practices for freezing popular foods. Storage times are for home freezers set at about 0°F.

BAKED GOODS

Low-moisture baked goods are ideal for freezing and maintain good quality for two to three months. Breads and rolls and even raw yeast doughs can be frozen. Doughs lose some yeast activity, so use a little extra yeast when preparing your dough if it is to be frozen. Properly wrapped pastry freezes well, baked or unbaked. Unbaked fruit pies can be frozen. Blackberry, blueberry, raspberry, and cranberry pies freeze and bake well. It is best to add a little oatmeal or some cookie crumbs to absorb moisture from fruits like apples or peaches. Both raw cookie dough and baked cookies freeze well. Freeze dough in cylinders ready to slice and bake. Freeze baked cookies in rigid containers with waxed paper between the layers. Tightly wrapped baked pound cakes, fruit cakes, and cake layers also freeze well. Decorated cakes with buttercream, high-fat icings, confectioners' sugar icing, and fudge icings freeze well, but cakes decorated with fondant, royal icing, or boiled icing do not. First, freeze the decorated cake until solid, then wrap it well and/or place it in a rigid container and return it to the freezer. To defrost, remove all the wrap and defrost it in the refrigerator overnight. Depending on the recipe, most cheesecakes freeze just fine.

EGGS

Egg whites can be frozen as is, but sugar or salt (about ½ teaspoon of salt or 1½ tablespoons of sugar for a cup of eggs) must be added to yolks or whole eggs to prevent gelation of the yolks. Whites, yolks, and whole eggs can be frozen in ice cube trays to create convenient portions, then dumped into zip-top freezer bags.

DAIRY PRODUCTS

Butter freezes and keeps well for about two to four months. Hard cheeses tend to crumble but are fine if used grated (and maintain their quality in the freezer for about six months). Cream cheese suffers texture-wise when frozen, but can be used for dips or anything that is beaten. Only heavy cream with about 40 percent butterfat can be frozen without separation. Whipped cream decoration can be frozen. Whip the cream, stir in ½ teaspoon of sugar per cup of cream, pipe into rosettes on trays, freeze solid, then package in a rigid container. Rich, high-fat mousses, like a heavy cream chocolate mousse, freeze well, while lean, beaten egg white–and–fruit mousses do not. Commercial ice creams and frozen yogurts have a quality freezer life of about one month.

VEGETABLES

Vegetables must be blanched to inactivate enzymes that speed browning. Cook the vegetable pieces in rapidly boiling, lightly salted water (about 1.2 percent salt to water volume improves retention of chlorophyll in green vegetables). Keep at a boil long enough for the center to reach 180°F. This will take from seconds to 4 minutes, depending on the vegetable size. Local extension services have charts detailing blanching times and preparation for different vegetables. Plunge into ice water to stop the cooking and leave in the ice water until thoroughly cool. Drain, and immediately freeze on trays or in freezer bags, squeezing out as much air as possible before sealing. Frozen vegetables are best cooked without first being thawed. Approximate home storage time for good quality is about eight months.

FRUITS

Fruits can be individually frozen on trays. They can also be sprinkled with dry sugar, or packed in syrup, or pureed and then put in zip-top freezer bags, or other freezer-safe containers, to freeze. Soft fruits, which make their own juice, can be sprinkled with dry sugar or frozen on trays. Firm fruits like peaches, apples, and apricots can be frozen in syrup with about 1,000 mg of vitamin C added per 4 cups of fruit to prevent browning. About the same amount of calcium from a calcium supplement, crushed, will make fruits firmer. My favorite way to freeze fruits like apples, peaches, and pears is to wash them thoroughly, core or pit them, slice into wedges, and then soak them briefly for two to three minutes in orange juice. Then drain the slices and place (not touching each other) on either a parchment-lined baking sheet or a nonstick baking sheet to freeze. When frozen, seal tightly in a zip-top freezer bag, squeezing out as much air as possible.

On Freezing

MEATS

Large pieces like beef roast or steaks have a quality freezer life of nine to twelve months. Separate individual steaks with waxed paper, then seal tightly in zip-top freezer bags, squeezing out as much air as possible. Ground meat has a maximum quality freezer life of three months. Pork fat is moderately unsaturated and can become off-tasting relatively fast, even when frozen. Ground pork and pork sausage keep well in the freezer for one to two months. Chops and roasts keep for four to six months.

POULTRY

Whole chickens and turkeys can be frozen for up to twelve months, while ducks and geese should be used within six months. Cut turkey pieces should be used within six months. Chicken pieces should be used within nine months.

FISH

Lean fish like cod, flounder, haddock, halibut, and pollack have about a 6-month quality freezer life, while a high-fat fish like salmon or ocean perch should be used within two months. To freeze a whole fish such as salmon, the fish must be gutted and rinsed well, then freezer paper can be stuffed into the cavity to preserve the shape. Whole fish are sometimes ice glazed—frozen on a tray, dipped in ice water, and refrozen several times to get an ice layer on the fish.

SAUCES, CUSTARDS, AND GRAVY

Mayonnaise separates upon freezing. Hollandaise sauce, on the other hand, freezes nicely. Defrost it over warm (not hot) water, with occasional whisking. Any sauces, custards, or gravy made with grain starches like flour or cornstarch freeze badly. The starch freezes into a firm sponge network while the liquid drains out, producing a dry sponge in a puddle. However, sauces, custards, or gravy made with root starches like arrowroot freeze beautifully.

HIGH-STARCH INGREDIENTS

Potatoes, pasta, rice, and barley become mushy when frozen, but mashed potatoes or pasta in a sauce freeze well.

SOUPS AND CASSEROLES

Most soups and casseroles freeze well. Remember that potatoes get mushy, and remember to thicken cream sauces with root starches like arrowroot powder or tapioca starch. If you wait until you thaw the soup to stir in milk, cream, or egg yolk, the risk of curdling is reduced.

On Freezing

Freezer Chart		
Food	Life (months)	Preparation or Problems
Baked Goods		
Breads and rolls	2–3	Cool quickly. Wrap tightly, then into freezer bag.
Frozen yeast dough	1	Add a little extra yeast when making dough.
Pastry—baked	2–3	Cool and package.
unbaked	1.5–2	Depending on the amount of preparation desired out of the freezer, either prepare as ready to bake, stack in pie pans with 2 layers of freezer paper, or store thin, flat, rolled-out rounds on cardboard with freezer paper between layers or shape into flattened 1-inch-thick rounds, wrap tightly in plastic wrap. Then put into freezer bag.*
Unbaked fruit pies	3–4	Make as usual except add 1 extra tbsp of flour, or 1 tbsp of tapioca, or ½ tbsp cornstarch to juicy fillings.** Or add a little oatmeal or some cookie crumbs to absorb moisture from higher moisture fruits like apples or peaches.
Cookies and raw dough	6	Freeze baked cookies in rigid containers with wax paper or freezer paper between layers. Freeze dough in cylinders ready to slice and bake. Or for drop cookies, drop on sheet or package bulk dough.

Food	Life (months)	Preparation or Problems
Baked Goods		
Fruit cakes	12	Wrap very tightly in plastic, then in foil.
Shortened cakes (standard white, yellow, chocolate, and pound)	2–4	It is best to freeze cakes and frosting separately. Cool well on a rack. Wrap (unfrosted layers, slices, whole cake) very tightly in plastic and then in foil.
Foam cakes: angel food	6 (egg-white cakes)	Cool cake well on a rack. If baked in a tube pan, fill hole with freezer paper so less air space. Put whole cake in a box to prevent crushing. If wrapping slices, put 2 pieces of freezer paper between slices. Wrap tightly and freeze.
sponge	4–6 (whole-egg cakes)	See above.
chiffon	2 (egg-yolk cakes)	See above.
Decorated cakes	2–4	Buttercream, high-fat icings, confectioners' sugar icing, and fudge frosting freeze well, but fondant, royal icing, or boiled icing do not. Place cake on a stiff foil or wax-paper-covered cardboard. First, freeze a decorated cake until solid to harden decorations, then wrap well and/or place in a rigid container and return to the freezer. To defrost, remove all wrap and defrost in refrigerator overnight.

On Freezing

Food	Life (months)	Preparation or Problems
Baked Goods		
Cheesecakes	1–3	Most freeze well—recipe dependent. May help to chill well or freeze before wrapping tightly.
Dairy		
Butter	2–4	Keep in original carton and put in freezer bag or mold into squares, pats, or desired shapes, wrap tightly in plastic wrap, foil, or freezer paper, or seal in moisture-vapor resistant containers.
Hard cheese	3–6	Wrap well. Tends to crumble, but okay to grate.
Semi-hard cheese	3	Cut into ½ or 1 lb size and wrap, then put in moisture-vapor resistant container. Tends to crumble, but okay to grate.
Cream cheese	1	Slight texture problems, but fine for dips and anything beaten.
Cream	1–2	Only heavy cream with 40% butterfat will freeze without separating.
Whipped cream	3–6	If going to whip cream, it is better to whip it to soft peaks, dollop spoonfuls on a sheet, and freeze. Then store in a zip-top bag or freezer container.

Food	Life (months)	Preparation or Problems
Dairy		
Milk	1–2	Use pasteurized, homogenized milk, place in moisture-vapor resistant containers. If in a wide-mouth container, leave ½-inch headspace for pint, 1 inch for a quart. If in a narrow-mouth container, leave 1½-inch headspace for pints and quarts. May separate, so stir well before using.
Ice cream and frozen yogurt	1 (in own pkg)	For storage longer than a month, if in original container, overwrap with freezer paper or plastic wrap, as original package is not moisture-vapor resistant.
Homemade ice cream		Doesn't freeze well—gets grainy (commercial products have extra milk solids and/or gelatin added to prevent that).
Eggs		
Whites	12	Freeze well—can freeze in ice cube trays and store in plastic freezer bag. Mix gently and strain through sieve before freezing. (2 tbsp mixture = 1 egg white)
Yolks and whole eggs	12	Stir yolks and whites to mix well. If yolks only, stir gently. Add 1½ tbsp sugar or ½ tsp salt per cup of either mixture. Strain through a sieve. Can freeze in ice cube trays: 3 tbsp whole egg in a cube = 1 whole egg. 1 tbsp yolk = 1 egg yolk. If freezing in a container, not trays, leave ½-inch headspace.

On Freezing

Food	Life (months)	Preparation or Problems
Meat		
Beef roasts and beef steaks	9–12	Separate individual steaks (or pieces) with wax paper, then seal tightly in zip-top freezer bags, squeezing out as much air as possible.
Lamb roasts	6–9	
Veal or pork roasts	4–6	
Ground meat	3	See above.
Beef, lamb, veal, and pork chops	4–6 4 (pork)	See above.
Ground pork and pork sausage	1–2	See above.
Poultry		
Whole chicken or turkey	12	Wrap in freezer wrap or freezer bags.
Chicken or turkey parts	9 (chicken) 6 (turkey)	Wrap in freezer wrap or freezer bags.
Whole duck or goose	6	Wrap in freezer wrap then in freezer bags.
Fish		
Low-fat fish: cod, cold flounder, haddock, halibut, and pollack	6–8	Dip for 20 seconds in brine (¼ cup salt to 1 quart water) to firm fish. Wrap in moisture-resistant paper or freezer bag.
High-fat fish: Salmon	2–3	Dip for 20 seconds in 2 tbsp ascorbic acid dissolved in 1 quart cold water (to control rancidity and flavor change). Wrap in freezer paper or freezer bag.

Food	Life (months)	Preparation or Problems
Fish		
Whole fish		Fish must be washed, descaled, gutted, and rinsed well, then freezer paper can be stuffed into the cavity to preserve the shape. Fish may also be glazed before freezing.***
Fruits	12	Fruits can be individually frozen on trays or sprinkled with dry sugar, packed in syrup, or pureed and put in zip-top freezer bags or other freezer-safe container. Soft fruits that make their own juice can be sprinkled with sugar or frozen on trays. Firm fruits like peaches, apples, and pears can be frozen in syrup with about 1000 mg of vitamin C added per 4 cups fruit, or quickly soaked in orange juice before freezing.
Vegetables	8–12	Must be blanched to inactivate enzymes that speed browning. Freeze in bags or freeze on trays and then put into bags. Preparation and blanching times vary with vegetable size. See University of Georgia Cooperative Extension for more.

Food	Life (months)	Preparation or Problems
Sauces		
Mayonnaise		Will not freeze without separating.
Hollandaise		Freezes well, reheat over warm (not hot) water, stirring occasionally.
Sauces, gravy, or custards with grain starches (like flour or cornstarch)	2–3	Freeze badly. Starch freezes in a sponge network while the liquid drains out. It is better to use arrowroot powder or tapioca starch as the thickener. For gravy, which also separates and curdles when thawed, it is better to either change the thickener (waxy flour [rice or corn], arrowroot powder, or tapioca starch can be used) or freeze the broth and make gravy right before serving.
Sauces or custards with root starches (like arrowroot powder or tapioca starch)	3–4	Freeze and thaw well. Package leaving headspace. Spices may change flavor with long storage so add before serving, not before freezing.
High-Starch Ingredients		
Potatoes, pasta, rice, and barley		Become mushy when frozen.

Food	Life (months)	Preparation or Problems
High-Starch Ingredients		
Mashed potatoes	0.5 (two weeks)	Freeze and thaw well. Make, pack in patties with 2 pieces of freezer paper between layers, or press in container with freezer paper between layers.
Pasta in sauce	4–6	Freezes well.
Soups and Casseroles	2–3	Most soups and casseroles freeze well. Remember, potatoes get mushy, so either puree them or leave them out to add later. Thicken cream soups with root starches like arrowroot powder or tapioca starch. If you wait until you thaw the soup to stir in milk, cream, or egg yolk, the risk of curdling is reduced.

* See King Arthur Flour blog *Make and Freeze Pie Crust—Saving Time—Sooner or Later.*
** See University of Georgia Cooperative Extension Service "Preserving Food: Freezing Prepared Foods" for more.
*** See University of Georgia Cooperative Extension Service "Preserving Food: Freezing Animal Products" for more.

Courtesy of the University of Georgia Cooperative Extension Service.
  "Preserving Food: Freezing Prepared Foods"
  "Preserving Food: Freezing Animal Products"
  "Preserving Food: Freezing Vegetables"
Courtesy of the USDA "Keep Food Safe! Food Safety Basics"
Courtesy of the USDA "Freezing and Food Safety"
Courtesy of the FDA "Refrigerator & Freezer Storage Chart"
Courtesy of the King Arthur Flour blog *Make and Freeze Pie Crust*

CHAPTER SEVEN

BAKING

I do all my baking on a large pizza stone that I keep on a shelf about eight inches above the oven floor. With baked goods, there is a fight between the dough getting warm and rising, and the heat from the top of the oven forming a crust, which holds the dough down. I preheat the oven for at least thirty minutes, then place my baked good on the hot stone, which gives it instant heat from the bottom. Since it is low in the oven, it gets a good head start on rising before the top starts to crust. The hot stone also provides even heat, which minimizes the effect of the oven's heating cycles. Also, with the even heat of the stone, I get a beautiful lightly browned bottom crust and never have to worry about the bottom burning.

FLOUR

The protein chemistry of flour dictates its best uses.

HIGH PROTEIN—MORE GLUTEN

When the cook adds water to flour and stirs, two proteins (glutenin and gliadin) join with water and each other to form gluten. These elastic bubble gum–like sheets of gluten are strong, and hold things together. They are also ideal for yeast-leavened products. Yeast oozes out a liquid that releases carbon dioxide gas and alcohol and inflates tiny bubbles in the dough. The elastic gluten sheets expand during this steady, gentle inflating process and the dough rises.

LOW PROTEIN—LESS GLUTEN

Baking powder and baking soda (chemical leaveners) work in an entirely different way than yeast. If you add hot water to baking powder, you will instantly see a great rush of fine bubbles. Strong sheets of gluten hold such a mass of bubbles down and actually interfere with this type of leavening.

You want a high-protein flour and a lot of gluten for yeast-leavened products, and for many egg-leavened baked goods, such as pâte à choux, popovers, and Yorkshire pudding. You also want gluten when you need strength, as for pasta and strudel dough that must be stretched thin, and puff pastry, Danish, and croissants that must be able to hold steam and puff apart where the fat has been.

Low-protein flour is excellent for baking powder– and baking soda–leavened products and anything that must be tender, like—pie crusts, cakes, biscuits, and quick breads.

HIGH PROTEIN, LOW PROTEIN— HOW CAN YOU TELL?

The Food and Drug Administration requires that flour be within 1 gram of the protein content stated on the bag. Previously, flour was labeled by cup portions. Bread flour was labeled 14 g protein per cup, unbleached 12 to 13 g per cup, national brand all-purpose 12 g per cup, Southern all-purpose 9 g per cup, and cake flour 8 g per cup. It was easy to tell that those labeled 13 to 14 g per cup were high-protein, while those labeled below 10 g per cup were low-protein.

Unfortunately, the portion amount for the new government regulations is ¼ cup, and nearly every flour on the market says 3 g protein per ¼ cup. The flour in the bag labeled 3 g per ¼ cup can really have from 8 g per cup to 16 g per cup. With the new regulations, you can tell absolutely nothing from the label about the protein content of the flour.

You know that bread flour is excellent for breads. You know that cake flour is excellent for cakes. And millers have traditionally made unbleached flour high in protein so you know that most unbleached flours will make light yeast breads. Self-rising flour is low in protein, but if you need a low-protein flour without leavening, you will need a Southern low-protein flour or to mix one-third cake flour or pregelatinized flour like Wondra or Shake & Blend (the flour sold in the cylinders like salt) with two-thirds national brand bleached all-purpose flour.

YEAST BREADS

A "SIMPLE" LOAF OF FRENCH BREAD

Actually, making a loaf of French bread can be anything but "simple." In Paris, at the Coupe du Monde de la Boulangerie—the Bakery World Cup—Team USA has won the bread or the overall title several times. I thought it was amazing that Team USA was baking better bread than the French and Italians, and agreed to participate.

Chef Didier Rosada coached our team for the 2002 and 2005 overall wins. Rosada and the great French bread master Professor Raymond Calvel place great emphasis on taste. How do you make one loaf of basic French bread taste better than another?

In Calvel's book, *The Taste of Bread*, he points out that selecting a flour with good carotenoid content and handling the dough so that you save these flavorful compounds are vital to the taste of bread. The wheat Calvel recommends is hard red winter wheat with a protein content of about 12 percent, not the higher-protein (13 to 14 percent) hard spring wheat.

I had always believed in really high-protein wheat for bread. I figured that the more protein, the more gluten, the lighter the bread. Then I had a class with Didier Rosada. He had us make loaves with the very high-protein hard spring wheat and the lower-protein hard winter wheat side by side. To my amazement, the final loaves made with the slightly lower-protein flour had as good or better volume than the ones made with the higher-protein flour! And the taste was wonderful!

I still have a lot to learn about gluten. Elastic sheets of gluten have two main characteristics: extensibility—how they stretch; and elasticity—how they spring back. The more extensible the gluten is, the more it can stretch, the more the loaf can rise. It may be that a wheat that forms more extensible gluten can make a loaf with as good or better rise than a higher-protein wheat that makes more elastic gluten.

In most supermarkets, you can now buy Gold Medal's Harvest King flour, a 100 percent hard red winter wheat unbleached flour (about 12 percent protein). (This is Professor Calvel's recommended flour.) It also has a trace of malt for good yeast activity. So, we have an outstanding bread flour available. Now, how can we preserve the precious flavorful carotenoid compounds it contains?

Unbleached hard red winter wheat produces doughs with a creamy color. Rosada had us stand around a large mixer and watch the dough as it was kneaded. The dough got whiter and whiter. As you knead, more and more oxygen combines with the dough. These flavorful carotinoid compounds oxidize and lose their color and the dough loses its flavor.

Can we get a good loaf with minimum kneading? Years ago, I talked to Dr. Carl Hoseney, one of the country's top starch and flour experts, about kneading. He startled me by saying that you really don't need to knead bread because when bread rises, it kneads itself on a molecule-by-molecule basis.

What does kneading do? As you work the dough, more proteins come in contact with other proteins and form more and more networks. In this way, kneading forms large, elastic sheets of gluten.

Hoseney pointed out that rising does this, too. When the liquid from the yeast touches a bubble in the dough, it releases carbon dioxide and alcohol—*poof*. It really is like someone blowing up bubble gum with tiny puffs. The dough moves. Proteins touch other proteins and cross-link. With every tiny rise of the dough, molecule by molecule, the dough "kneads" itself—no need to knead!

MUCH DEPENDS ON TEMPERATURE

Professor Calvel stresses that dough temperature has an important effect on oxidation during mixing and the accompanying flavor loss. Average bakery mixing temperatures vary between 75°F and 77°F. Deterioration of flavor is much more pronounced at dough-mixing temperatures between 78°F and 80°F. And bread flavor is greatly enhanced by lower mixing temperatures in the range of 70°F to 73°F. So, we have our ideal mixing (kneading) temperature, between 71°F and 73°F.

Ideal dough temperature depends on the situation. A sourdough starter where you are trying to beg wild yeast to grow should be about 80°F, a temperature where the yeast has maximum activity. A good temperature for a flavorful baker's yeast preferment like a sponge, biga, or poolish is about 70°F. At this temperature, both yeast and bacteria can have some activity, producing a very flavorful starter. For a good rise, both in bulk dough and shaped dough, you want a warmer temperature: 76°F.

In the following recipes, I have incorporated much of what I have learned about flour, kneading, and temperature. I follow the basic formula I learned from Professor Calvel and then take you step-by-step to make beautiful baguettes.

In a home kitchen and with our minimum kneading, I think that if you just take an assessment of temperatures (room temperature, flour temperature, and water temperature), you can make some educated guesses. You can always add a few ice cubes to several cups of water, get it to your desired temperature, and then remove the ice.

For the purist, here is the professional formula for calculating the water temperature from Wayne Gisslen's *Professional Baking:*

Desired dough temperature times 3, minus the sum of the flour temperature plus the room temperature plus machine friction will give you the temperature you need for the water. This formula uses 20°F/11°C as the machine friction value.

POOLISH AND BAGUETTES

A poolish is a baker's yeast preferment for wonderful flavored breads. Poolishes contain a small amount of yeast with equal weights of liquid and flour, and no salt.

Before you begin, take some temperatures with an instant-read thermometer: your flour, faucet water, and the kitchen counter or table. Ideally, you want to find a place for the poolish mixture to rise that is 70°F. You want your mixing temperature about 72°F, and you need a warmer spot (76°F) for the dough to rise.

POOLISH

⅛ teaspoon instant yeast (also sold as rapid-rise or
  quick-rise yeast)
½ cup plus 1 teaspoon water (about 68°F)
1 cup minus 2 tablespoons (4.19 ounces/119 g) spooned
  and leveled Gold Medal Harvest King flour

In a medium bowl, stir the yeast into the water, then stir in the flour in two batches. Stir or beat with a hand mixer for about 1 minute, until smooth. Scrape the mixture into a clean, wide-mouth quart jar. The temperature of the mixture should be about 70°F. Cover and allow to stand for 6 to 12 hours to ripen. Fine bubbles should cover the surface of a ripe poolish. You can even see bubbles break on the surface. If the poolish is past its prime—has risen and collapsed—there will be a foam line on the glass above the current poolish level. Use immediately.

This ripening time is totally dependent on the amount of yeast and the temperature. It may take a time or two and playing with the amounts of yeast and temperature to get the poolish where you would like it for your schedule. My poolish was ripe and ready to use in my baguette recipe in a little over 6 hours.

BAGUETTES

1 recipe Poolish (above)

1 cup water (about 68°F), plus 2 to 4 tablespoons as needed

¼ teaspoon plus ⅛ teaspoon instant yeast (also sold as rapid-rise or quick-rise yeast)

1¾ teaspoons salt (sea salt, if possible)

¹⁄₁₆ teaspoon (10 to 50 mg) ascorbic acid (vitamin C; see Note)

3 cups (13.5 ounces/382.7 g) spooned and leveled Gold Medal Harvest King flour

Oil, for the bowl and counter

Nonstick spray

Pour the poolish into the bowl of a stand mixer. (Ideal mixing temperature is about 72°F.) Add the water, yeast, salt, and ascorbic acid. Using the paddle attachment, mix for a few seconds on the lowest speed, then add 2 cups of the flour and mix for a few seconds. Add the rest of the flour and mix on low for about 1 minute, then mix on the second speed for about 2 minutes. The dough should be soft, on the edge of sticky. Add a tablespoon or so of more water if needed.

Oil your hands and very lightly oil a large bowl. Place the dough in the oiled bowl, cover, and allow to rise for 1 hour. (The ideal temperature for rising is about 76°F.)

After 1 hour, "fold" the dough. (The directions that follow are essentially (with a few differences) those of Jeffrey Hamelman, the author of *Bread*, for "folding" instead of "punching down." Folding develops a little more gluten and leaves the dough more aerated than punching down does.) There is an excellent video on the King Arthur flour website on shaping, featuring Jeffrey Hamelman, so you can see firsthand how to shape a baguette. (At www.kingarthurflour.com, look under the heading "Learn" for "Videos," then "Professional Techniques," where you'll find the video "Techniques for the Professional Baker 4: Shaping.") The easiest way to learn is to watch someone do it, and you can do that now with the King Arthur flour video.

Using an oiled paper towel, very lightly oil a clean countertop. Dump the dough out onto the oiled surface so the smooth top of the dough is now on the bottom. Allow it to spread out as much as it will. Pick up the dough on the left side, lifting up about one-third of the dough, and gently fold it across to the right, trapping some air as you make the fold. Allow it to spread for a few seconds, then lift up about one-third of the right side of the dough and bring it across to the left. Again, give the dough a few seconds to spread. Now pick up the bottom edge of the dough and bring about one-third of it up and across to the top. After it settles, pick up the top edge, lift about one-third of it up, and bring it across toward you. Place the dough back in the bowl, turning it over so that the smooth top that was against the counter is back on top. Cover and allow to rise for another hour.

Lift the dough out and place it on the lightly oiled counter, smooth-side up. Divide the dough in half. Working with one half at a time, use both hands in a cupping motion to tuck the sides slightly under to create a smooth top. By tucking the dough into a tight, smooth round, you create a covering to better hold gases. With both hands, grab the sides of the round and stretch it sideways into an oval. Let it spring back slightly, then pull it out again. Cover the oval with plastic wrap and repeat with the second portion of dough, then leave them on the counter for about 20 minutes. The relaxed dough is now much easier to shape.

To shape the baguettes, cup one oval piece of dough with both hands on top of the loaf with your palms facing down, fingers spread out behind the loaf on either end and thumbs in front of the loaf. Press your thumbs into the dough closest to you and down against the counter. This pulls or tucks part of the bottom half of the dough under. At the same time, with your fingers, pull the top of the dough tight and up and over, forward (toward yourself and your thumbs), lightly pressing the dough to seal it. Now move your thumbs down slightly and press down and in/under again, pulling the top forward with your fingers to knead and tuck again. Repeat this motion two or three times, until the loaf is stretched taut and well tucked in. The loaf will lengthen as you stretch and tuck and may be long enough if you have pulled your hands outward in the process. If not, lengthen the loaf by placing both hands, spread out, palms down, on top of the center of the loaf. Then simultaneously push away against the counter with your right hand and pull toward your body with your left, pulling the dough out in opposite directions. Repeat this pulling once or twice more, if necessary. Pinch the bottom seam together. Repeat to form the second oval into a baguette.

Spray a double-trough French baguette pan with nonstick spray. Place the loaves, seam-side down, in the pan, cover with a floured smooth-surfaced towel or plastic wrap, and allow to rise for 1 to 1½ hours. (The ideal temperature for rising is about 76°F.)

After the loaves have been rising for about 45 minutes, arrange a shelf in the lower third of the oven, place a baking stone on it, and preheat the oven to 460°F. Place a few clean small rocks (1 to 2 inches each) in a metal pan with 1- to 2-inch sides and place the pan on the floor of the oven near the front of the stove. You are going to pour about 2 cups of boiling water over the rocks just before you put the bread in the oven to create a steam bath. You want a good steam-filled oven for the bread to go in. This steam will condense on the dough to keep it moist and allow a good "oven rise."

Place about 2½ cups of water in a saucepan with a long handle on a back burner and bring it to a low simmer. When the loaves have risen, turn the heat up on the water and bring it to a boil. VERY CAREFULLY—MAKE SURE THAT YOUR HANDS ARE OUT OF THE WAY OF THE STEAM THAT WILL BURST UP—pour the boiling water into the pan of hot rocks. Close the oven door to allow the oven to fill with steam.

It is imperative to slash the loaves so that they can rise rapidly in the hot oven. To slash the loaves, you need a single-edge razor blade or a clean X-ACTO knife. (Bakers use a tool called a lame, pronounced *lahm*, that looks like a razor blade at the end of a small stick. These are available from King Arthur.) Slashes should be made by holding the lame at about a 30-degree angle to the top surface of the bread so you are slashing a thin flap of dough, not straight down into the dough. For dough laying on a table vertically, start at the top of the baguette (farthest from you) and work down the baguette (toward you). These slashes are all straight down the centerline lengthwise of the dough, about 4 to 5 inches long, starting about ¼ inch to the right of the centerline, crossing the centerline and ending ¼ inch to the left of the centerline. At a 30-degree angle to the top surface of the dough, make a slash down the center about 5 inches long. Each slash should overlap the previous slash by about one-quarter of its length. So, start a little over an inch from the bottom of the first slash, close to it and parallel to it, and make another 5-inch slash down the center of the baguette. Continue in this way to slash all the way down the center of the loaf. All slashes should start ¼ inch to the right of the lengthwise centerline of the baguette and end ¼ inch to the left of the lengthwise centerline of the baguette.

Place the pan with the loaves on the hot baking stone in the oven. Bake until well browned, about 25 minutes. Place the loaves on a wire rack to cool. Serve warm or at room temperature.

Makes 2 baguettes

NOTE: You can buy vitamin C powder at Whole Foods, or you can cut a 500-mg vitamin C tablet into fourths, crush one fourth, and use a pinch of this.

NOTE: For more information about French bread and starters, see *BakeWise*.

YEAST BREAD PROBLEMS

Dough does not rise or bread is very heavy

Poor gluten formation or dead yeast is the problem. If the dough is elastic and springy, you have a yeast problem. If the dough tears and pulls apart easily, you do not have adequate gluten.

Possible causes of poor gluten formation: flour low in gluten-forming proteins; too much sugar (over 1 tablespoon of sugar per cup of flour reduces gluten formed); flour coated with fat before the liquid was added; lack of mechanical action (working of dough). Ingredients that aid gluten formation: vitamin C and a small amount of salt.

Possible causes of damage to yeast: dissolving dry yeast in water that is too cold; mixing yeast with ingredients that are too hot (above about 130°F); too much salt; too much sugar; certain spices like dry mustard or large amounts of spices. Ingredients that enhance yeast activity: malt, malted flour, barley malt syrup, dairy products, small amounts of spices like ginger, cinnamon, and nutmeg.

Dough texture is different when a different flour is used

The higher the protein content of plain white flour, the greater the amount of water it absorbs. It is not humidity that determines how much water a flour absorbs; it is the amount of these gluten-forming proteins it contains. Higher-protein flour makes more gluten and lighter yeast breads.

Bread stales rapidly

Staling occurs faster at refrigerator temperatures than at room temperature. Freeze bread or keep it at room temperature. Ingredients that slow staling: emulsifiers like those in egg yolks, cinnamon in small amounts, and pureed raisins.

Sweet dough is heavy

Too much sugar (use a maximum of 2 tablespoons of sugar per cup of flour) prevents gluten formation and makes bread heavy. Glutenin and gliadin combine with sugar, and you don't get much gluten formed.

Acidity

Acidic ingredients make proteins set (cook) faster. This is very important in baking. If cookie batter sets faster, it limits the spread of the cookies. In cakes, normal baking with an acidic batter will produce a cake with a finer texture. It is vital to set a batter quickly when baking at high altitudes.

In pastry making, acidity cuts some of the gluten strands to tenderize the dough and make it easier to roll, but acidity also makes the crust set faster and hold its shape better.

In muffins, faster cooking means the outside will set while the center is still juicy and rising, to give you a better peak, especially at 400°F to 425°F.

STEAM-LEAVENED

Years ago, in the Oak Room, a great, dark, old dining room that had been a men-only section of Dayton's Department Store in Minneapolis, I ate the most spectacular popover I had ever seen. It was a huge explosion of crispness. It was delicious. It was wonderful. I had never had anything like it. I never knew that a popover could be so big. The only popovers I had seen before were like large, puffy muffins—nothing like this.

Susan Dietrich, a top Minneapolis food professional, was generously leading a group I was with on a tour of great food finds in Minneapolis and took us to the Oak Room. Dayton's has since become a Marshall Fields and then Macy's, but—hurrah!—the Oak Room still made those great popovers. Executive chef Marie Harris assured me that popovers were not only thriving at the Oak Room, but they had been expanded to a suburban store as well. Chef Harris said they served hundreds of popovers over the holidays.

After experiencing the Oak Room's, I just had to learn how to make big popovers. I discovered early on in my popover journey that the recipe was only part of the secret to huge popovers. Sadly, I learned that as of 2017, the Oak Room I visited at the downtown Minneapolis location is no longer there, as that Macy's is closed. The secret of the big popovers lives on, as you can see.

Popovers are steam-leavened. You have to get the batter hot fast to produce steam to inflate a strong, balloonlike protein structure of eggs and flour.

And then you have the great oven fight. The batter or

dough needs to rise before heat from the top of the oven causes a crust to form and hold the batter down. In years gone by, fail-safe popovers were put into a cold oven and then the oven was turned on. The heating element in ovens of the past was at the bottom. So, with a blast of heat from the bottom and no heat from the top to hold the dough down, the popover beautifully exploded to impressive heights.

Nowadays, however, heat comes from all over in modern ovens. They are designed to preheat fast—often in 10 minutes or less. If you put something in a cold oven and turn the heat on, all the heating units in the oven come on full blast and can burn any food to a crisp. So what can you do to get heat from the bottom?

My solutions are to use a baking stone and absolutely never open the oven door until the popovers are totally done. I place the stone on a shelf in the lower third of the oven, wanting as much distance from the top of the oven as possible. I preheat the oven to 475°F and get the stone really hot. The even heat of the stone prevents the popovers from burning on the bottom. I put the popovers in the oven, then after 9 minutes, I turn the oven down to 425°F; the stone stays hot but the heating elements go off. Then, after another 7 minutes, I turn the oven down to 325°F and bake the popovers for 25 minutes to dry them so that they won't fall when I take them out.

Having the batter as warm as possible is another secret to success. Popovers expand best if the flour is fully hydrated. The proteins and starch in the flour take a little time to fully soak in the liquid, so most popover recipes tell you to let the batter stand for 30 minutes to 1 hour before baking. This means that your batter will be at room temperature going into the oven. To get a warmer batter, I let the flour and the milk—not the assembled batter—stand for 1 hour. Then I stir warm eggs in well, and finally, I heat the batter by pouring in boiling cream. This won't make the eggs cook because of the starch in the batter (in the flour).

I have heated my pan—so I have a hot pan, hot batter, and a hot stone in a hot oven. The batter builds up steam fast. I have used high-protein bread flour, so I have a strong protein network with the flour and the eggs to hold the steam. I also have used milk instead of water for a little extra protein and beautiful browning (and, with the cream, great taste). The popovers explode to great heights. I also replace some whole eggs with egg whites, which are a great drying agent for drier, crisper popovers. With these cooking times, the heat stays on long enough to firmly set the puffy popovers.

I just love these popovers. I hope you do, too. Bring on the butter, and let's eat!

SHIRLEY'S MILE-HIGH POPOVERS

These popovers are deep brown and crusty and oh so good! They deserve the best butter that you can buy.

The true secret of big popovers is to make sure that everything—the pan, the baking stone, the batter, everything—is as warm as you can get it, when the batter goes into the oven.

What This Recipe Shows

Letting the milk and flour stand for an hour or so ensures that the flour is fully hydrated.

Adding hot cream to warm the batter just before it goes in the oven helps the batter to heat quickly, producing steam for a great rise.

A high-protein flour is crucial for a strong egg-flour network to hold the steam.

The hot stone is vital in providing instant even heat from the bottom to make the batter explode into great puffs.

Egg whites make drier, crisper popovers.

5 large eggs
Hot water
1½ cups whole milk
1¾ cups spooned and leveled Pillsbury bread flour
⅓ cup heavy cream
¾ teaspoon finely ground sea salt
Nonstick spray

In a bowl of very hot tap water, place the eggs (still in their shell) to warm. After a while, drain and cover again with very hot tap water.

In a heavy saucepan, warm the milk until it feels warm to the touch. Place the flour in a large bowl (if you have a large measuring cup with a spout, that will be great for pouring the batter later). With a fork or whisk, beat in the milk a little at a time to prevent lumps from forming. Allow the flour-milk mixture to stand at room temperature for at least 1 hour.

After the flour mixture has been standing for about 15 minutes, arrange a shelf in the lower third of the oven, set a baking stone on it, and preheat the oven to 475°F. If you think your oven runs cooler, turn it to 500°F. It is important that the oven be very hot. After the flour mixture has stood for at least 1 hour, place a popover pan on the baking stone in the oven to heat.

Separate 3 eggs, saving the whites and discarding or storing the yolks for another use. Beat the 2 whole eggs and the 3 egg whites together. Beat in about ½ cup of the flour mixture and then beat the egg mixture into the flour mixture.

In a small saucepan, heat the cream almost to a boil. Sprinkle the salt over the batter and whisk in the hot cream. Pull the hot popover pan out of the oven. (I like to place the pan over the sink while I fill it.) Spray one cup of the popover pan well with nonstick spray and immediately pour the batter into that cup, filling it slightly more than three-quarters full. Repeat, spraying and then filling each cup. This batch of batter is exactly enough to fill all 6 cups. Place the popover pan on the hot stone in the oven and bake for 9 minutes. Do *not* open the oven. Turn down the heat to 425°F and bake for 7 minutes more. Do *not* open the oven. Turn down the oven to 325°F and leave the popovers in for 20 to 25 minutes more so they can dry out. Dump the popovers out onto a wire rack to cool briefly. Serve immediately, with really good butter and preserves. You can make these several hours ahead and rewarm them at 300°F for 5 minutes. When they are completely cool, you can seal them in heavy-duty zip-top freezer bags and freeze. Reheat in a 300°F oven for about 5 minutes.

Makes 6 large popovers

PASTRY

PIE CRUST PROBLEMS

Not crisp enough

I like to prebake my pie crust, and I bake it between two identical pie pans. I do not like to punch holes in the crust. My favorite pans have holes that prevent the crust from bubbling up from air trapped between the crust and the pan. I initially bake the crust upside down (for about 20 minutes at 425°F). This will lengthen the sides rather than shorten them. Then I remove the pan that is covering the bottom of the crust and bake the crust upside down again for about 5 minutes to dry and crisp the bottom. I then replace the pan, turn the crust over, remove the inside pan, and bake the crust for 5 minutes more to dry and crisp the inside. The crust is now thoroughly dry. I brush the inside with egg white and return it to the oven for about 2 minutes to cook the egg white, forming a shield that will keep my crust crisp when the filling is added.

Crusts are tough

Too much gluten. Work the fat into the flour well to grease the gluten-forming proteins (glutenin and gliadin) so they cannot join together with water and each other to form gluten.

The addition of sugar can reduce gluten, as can acidic ingredients. Limiting available water limits gluten, too.

Crusts are crumbly

Too little gluten. Do not work the fat in so well before the liquid is added.

Crusts are not flaky

The fat is too warm and cut too fine. Large, cold, flat pieces of fat that are cold enough and large enough to not melt instantly serve as "spacers" to separate layers of dough just long enough for them to begin to set. The fat then melts, and steam comes from the dough and puffs the layers of dough apart for flakiness.

An easy way to get these pieces of fat for flakiness is to cut a stick of butter lengthwise in half, then lengthwise in half again so that you have 4 "logs." Cut each of these logs crosswise into 3 pieces so that you have short logs ½ inch square at the cross section and about 1½ inches long. Toss these butter logs with flour and salt and place in the freezer for 10 minutes. Dump the cold butter-flour mixture onto a clean counter and roll over the mixture with a rolling pin. The butter may stick to the pin; simply scrape it off. Pile the mixture together and roll over it again. Do this three times for wonderful large, flat pieces of butter. Scrape the mixture back into the bowl, chill for 10 minutes, then work in enough sour cream to make a dough. This makes a dough so flaky that it is like puff pastry. Bake rolled-out dough between two pie pans, upside down (see the above section "Not crisp enough").

Super-Puff Puff Pastry

High-protein flour makes more gluten, which makes higher puff pastry. However, a pastry chef may say it is impossible to roll out high-protein-flour doughs because the gluten is so strong. Gluten is not only composed of glutenin and gliadin—its third ingredient is water. When you work a dough, more and more of the flour proteins (glutenin and gliadin) link with water to form gluten. This removes the water from the dough. Not only have you formed strong, tough gluten, you have dried out the dough. Now this dry, tough dough is impossible to roll out big enough to make folds for puff pastry.

But if you add water and keep this dough soft, it can be rolled out. How can you add water to this already-made dough? Directions for making puff pastry tell you to brush off the excess flour after you roll the dough out. If you not only brush off the excess flour, but also brush the dough with ice water before each fold, you can keep the dough soft and easy to roll. This will not only allow you to make puff pastry with a high-protein flour for a higher puff, it also provides more water for more steam in the hot oven, for super-high puff pastry.

CAKES, QUICK BREADS, AND MUFFINS

In my early days of cake baking, I would go crazy when I had followed a recipe from a "good cookbook" exactly and it did not come out right. It was an enormous waste of time and ingredients.

With my zeal for research, I dug into the problem. I learned quickly that I had not done anything wrong; it was a bad recipe. To my horror, there are hundreds of bad recipes out there. How do professional bakers spot bad recipes? I sought and found "insider information." Here are some of the bakers' tips for correcting bad cake recipes.

LEAVENING RULE

Many bad recipes have too much leavening. If you have too much leavening, the bubbles get too big, float to the top, and pop, and the cake will fall or be very heavy. Cakes, muffins, and quick breads should have no more than 1¼ teaspoons baking powder per cup of flour, or ¼ teaspoon baking soda per cup of flour.

PERCENTAGE GUIDES

You can use baker's percentage guides to compare amounts of ingredients in a recipe. For example, compare the amount of fat to the amount of flour. The baker's percentage guide for fat says that the weight of the fat should be 30 percent to 60 percent of the weight of the flour. This percentage guide for fat can be very helpful. If the weight of the fat in your cake is only about 30 perecent of the weight of the flour, the cake will be very lean, not rich at all. On the other hand, if the weight of the fat is 70 percent the weight of the flour, the cake may be greasy. You should cut some of the fat.

Baker's percentage guides for sugar run all over the place, depending on the type of flour and the type of fat being used, so the general guide for sugar—that the weight of the sugar can run from 50 percent to 140 percent of the weight of the flour—covers too wide a range to be very helpful.

BASIC FORMULAS
FOR BALANCING CAKES

Cake, muffin, and quick bread recipes must be in balance. The sugar and fat are tenderizers—they make things tender and fall apart. The flour and eggs contain proteins that hold things together. They provide the structure, the toughening. For a successful cake, you need a balance of tenderizing or tearing-apart ingredients and toughening or holding-together ingredients. Master cake bakers always start with and stay relatively close to these formulas:

Regular Cakes
Weight of sugar equal to or less than weight of flour (including any added starch)
Weight of eggs (egg yolks + whole eggs, not the shell) equal to or greater than weight of fat (oil + butter + fat in cream)
Weight of liquid (milk + whole eggs + cream minus cream fat) equal to weight of flour

High-Ratio Cakes
(Many cakes fall into this category because we like a high ratio of sugar; I prefer this formula.)
Weight of sugar equal to or greater than weight of flour (including any added starch)
Weight of eggs (includes yolks plus whole egg, not weight of the shell) equal to weight of fat (includes butter, oil, and fat in cream)
Weight of liquid (including weight of whole eggs and weight of cream minus the weight of the cream fat) equal to or greater than weight of sugar

COMBINING AND BAKING

Having the right amounts of butter, flour, eggs, and sugar is only half the battle. The way you combine ingredients and bake the batter can have a huge effect on the texture and structure of your cakes and muffins. Here is part two of the story.

BEATING BUBBLES INTO FAT CREATES A LIGHT CAKE

There are many techniques for mixing cake batters, but the two most common are the creaming method and the two-stage method, also called the blending method. The method you choose depends in part on the style of cake you want. Some people like an extremely light, well-aerated cake, while others prefer a more velvety, tender texture and will accept a heavier cake in exchange.

Creaming Method

If you want a light cake, use the creaming method. The key to a light cake is to trap lots of tiny bubbles in the butter or shortening and then let the leaveners (baking powder or baking soda) go to work enlarging those bubbles. In the creaming method, you beat the butter, add the sugar, and continue beating until the mixture is pale and fluffy. To start creaming, the butter should not be too cold or too hot. Your finger should leave a small imprint in the butter. You should take it out of the refrigerator ½ to 1 hour before it is needed. Most home bakers give this step short shrift, not aerating the batter fully. It takes at least 5 minutes (some bakers say 10 minutes), but you can't let the butter get so soft that it melts or you'll lose the bubbles. To help keep the butter cool, chill the bowl and beaters beforehand and either cut the slightly softened butter into slices or you can even grate the butter on the cheese section of a grater. You can also stop beating when the butter starts to soften too much and put the bowl in the freezer for 5 minutes, if needed, before continuing.

When the butter and sugar are very light, beat in the eggs one at a time so the batter doesn't get lumpy. Bruce Healy, author of *The Art of the Cake*, established that this step doesn't add any volume, so you only need to blend until the eggs are well incorporated.

The last step is to stir in part of the well-sifted dry ingredients, then half the liquid, more of the dry mixture, the rest of the liquid, and finally the remaining dry mixture. The alternating additions of dry ingredients and liquid ensure that the batter blends evenly. There's a potential pitfall: development of too much gluten, which makes the cake tough or leads to tunnels. The first addition of flour gets well coated with fat and doesn't form gluten, but once the liquid is added, uncoated flour proteins in the next addition of dry ingredients can combine with the liquid to form tough gluten. To minimize this, I like to add most of the dry ingredients in that first addition. Once the liquid is added, you must avoid overmixing in order to limit gluten formation.

Two-Stage Method

If a cake with a velvety, dissolving texture is your heart's desire, the two-stage method is for you. First you blend all the dry ingredients, all the fat, and a small amount of the total liquid and then you add the remaining liquid. This method lets the fat coat all the flour proteins and prevents the formation of gluten, producing an incredibly tender cake—so tender that it falls apart in your mouth. This dissolving texture gives the illusion of lightness, but in fact, cakes made by this method are heavier than those made by the creaming method.

MUFFIN METHOD

For casual quick breads and muffins, which aren't intended to be light and airy, use the muffin method: combine the dry ingredients in one bowl, the wet ingredients in another, and then stir them together. In contrast to the creaming method, the key here is not to stir too long or too vigorously, since stirring flour and liquid together forms gluten, and that would make the muffins or quick bread tough.

How to Tweak a Recipe

I once found a recipe in a magazine for Golden Layer Cake and studied its ratios before trying it out. First, I checked the leavening, which was perfect—1 teaspoon of baking powder per cup of flour. However, the recipe called for 1¼ cups of sugar, which is about 8½ ounces, and 2¼ cups of flour, about 11 ounces. The weight of the sugar is less than the weight of the flour, when it is supposed to be equal or more. This indicates that these layers may be dry.

I could have improved this cake just by increasing the amount of sugar relative to the flour, but I made additional changes to make the cake even moister:

- I increased the sugar a little to 1½ cups (10.16 ounces) and decreased the flour a little to 2 cups, so the weight of the sugar is a little greater than the weight of the flour (8.47 ounces) plus the weight of the potato starch (1.5 ounces) (9.97 ounces total).
- I switched to self-rising flour because normally it is a slightly lower-protein flour, producing a tenderer cake, and the leavening is perfectly distributed throughout it so the cake will have perfect texture. Since self-rising flour contains leavening, using it allows me to cut one ingredient as well.
- I changed to ½ cup heavy cream plus ¾ cup buttermilk because I love the taste of cream and buttermilk in baked goods. If you whip the cream and fold it in, it lightens the cake. I wanted the buttermilk for its acidity, which helps set the cake, and for lightness, because it makes more steam than cream does.

- I wanted to make the layers really moist, so I cut some of the butter and used some oil instead. Oil coats the flour proteins and prevents their forming gluten, which ties up water, removing it from the cake.
- I also added some potato starch, whose huge granules hold moisture.
- Finally, I added more flavoring by using vanilla bean paste, which I added to the fat for even distribution throughout the cake.

MOIST GOLDEN LAYER CAKE

These cake layers are moist, tender, light, and wonderful!

What This Recipe Shows

Substituting around 10 percent potato starch for flour adds huge starch granules, which hold moisture.

Using some oil, which coats flour proteins better than butter, ensures less gluten and more moisture.

A high amount of sugar reduces gluten formation for more moisture.

Vanilla bean paste gives more intense flavor.

Buttermilk adds acidity to set the cake, as well as flavor and liquid, which creates steam for lightness.

Egg yolks provide emulsifiers for a smooth texture.

Self-rising flour ensures even distribution of leavening.

1½ cups (10.16 ounces) sugar

Nonstick spray

6 tablespoons (¾ stick/3 ounces) butter (contains
    2.4 ounces fat), right out of the refrigerator, cut
    into teaspoon-size pieces

⅓ cup (2.5 ounces) vegetable oil

1 tablespoon vanilla bean paste

4 large egg yolks (2.6 ounces)

2 large eggs (3.5 ounces)

2 cups (8.47 ounces) low-protein self-rising flour

¼ cup (1½ ounces) potato starch

¼ teaspoon finely ground sea salt

¾ cup (6.2 ounces) buttermilk

½ cup (4 ounces) heavy cream (contains
    1.4 ounces fat)

Arrange a shelf in the lower third of the oven, set a baking stone or heavy baking sheet on it, and preheat the oven to 350°F. You can skip the baking stone or sheet if you have a small oven. If you have a convection oven, set it to 325°F.

Place a mixer bowl and whisk attachment in the freezer to chill. Place the sugar in the freezer to chill.

Spray two 9-inch round metal cake pans (heavy, light-colored aluminum pans work best) with nonstick spray and line the bottoms with parchment paper circles cut to fit. (I lightly spray the top of the parchment, too.)

Take the butter out of the refrigerator about ½ hour before using it. It should be slightly soft (a finger makes a small, not-too-deep impression).

In the cold mixer bowl using the cold whisk on low speed, beat the butter to soften it and get to the fluffy stage. Add the sugar and continue beating. This should take 3 to 5 minutes. If the butter appears to be melting too much, put the bowl in the freezer to get it cold again. If the butter is too cold, however, it won't cream properly. Drizzle in the oil and continue to beat. Beat in the vanilla bean paste. Again, place the bowl in the freezer for a few minutes to chill if it is not cold. Beat the egg yolks in one at a time, then beat in the eggs, one at a time.

Sift the flour, potato starch, and salt together into a medium bowl. Then whisk or beat the three dry ingredients together thoroughly. With the mixer on low speed, slowly add most of the flour mixture. Drizzle in the buttermilk and cream. (For extra lightness, whip the cream on high speed in a cold bowl with cold beaters, only until soft peaks form, then fold it into the batter.) Pour the batter into the prepared pans and smooth it out. Pat the bottom of each pan firmly several times with your hand to bring any air bubbles to the top to pop. Place the pans on the baking stone or baking sheet, if you are using one, in the oven and bake until a toothpick inserted into the center of each cake comes out dry, about 20 minutes. Place the pans on a wire rack and let cool for 10 minutes, then remove the cakes from the pans to finish cooling. The layers may be cut in half horizontally to form 4 layers, if desired.

Makes one 9-inch double-layer cake

CAKE PROBLEMS

Any number of factors can lead to trouble with cakes or muffins, and that makes it hard to identify the real cause—or causes. Here is a list of several cake and muffin problems and a few of their likely causes.

Falling

Too much leavening. The bubbles get big, float to the top, and *pop*! There goes your leavening. Keep the leavening close to 1 teaspoon of baking powder or ¼ teaspoon of baking soda per cup of flour.

Cake or muffins are heavy

Batter was undermixed; oven too hot; too much sugar or fat (or both).

Fall in center only

Probably not thoroughly cooked. Cook slightly longer, or cook at a lower temperature for a longer time.

Tough or spongy

If just tough, too much gluten. If spongy, too much egg.

Cake grainy

Oven not hot enough; poor mixing; batter not acidic enough.

Cake not level

With cakes, the goal is a level top that's as flat as a skating rink, while muffins, in my ideal world, should peak like a volcano. In addition to oven temperature, choosing the right baking pan can help. Make sure your oven temperature isn't too high.

Heavy, dull, light-colored aluminum pans absorb less heat, and this makes them the best choice for level cakes. Gray non-stick pans work well, too. A dark pan, which absorbs more heat, can set the outside of the cake before the inside gets hot. The wet center will continue to rise, and you may end up with a peaked cake. For muffins to peak, gray pans are excellent. Black pans would also work, but if you're not careful, they'll burn the muffins.

Flat muffins

A higher baking temperature (400°F to 425°F) is key for a volcanic muffin. In this case, you want to encourage the outside to set fast and let the inside keep rising. If the muffins brown too fast, reduce the oven temperature for the last 10 minutes of baking. Many muffin recipes say to preheat the oven to 325°F or 350°F, but you won't get good peaks at these temperatures.

More acidic batter will set faster, allowing the edges to set while the center is wet and can continue to rise.

Tunnels

Oven is too hot; batter overmixed; too much batter in the pan.

Cakes, quick breads, or muffins are dry

Too much egg white (use 2 yolks for 1 whole egg), too much flour, or not enough sugar or fat. Substitute ½ cup of oil for ½ cup (1 stick) of butter in the recipe.

Coarse texture

Oven temperature and pan color can make the difference. When a cake bakes, the air bubbles you've beaten into the fat expand until the egg and flour proteins coagulate, the flour's starch gelatinizes, and the cake's structure sets. Larger bubbles mean an airy, coarser-textured cake; smaller bubbles give a finer texture but also a denser cake. For finer-textured cakes, try a slightly higher baking temperature (350°F).

This will set the cake sooner and keep the bubbles from getting too big. For a lighter cake with a slightly more open texture, a slower oven (325°F) will help. The cake will need a few more minutes in the oven, but the lower temperature will give the bubbles more time to swell before the batter sets.

Cakes with beaten egg whites fall

When you beat egg whites, their proteins unwind and join loosely. You can think of them as partially "cooked," and they are no longer available to be a major part of the cake's expanding structure. Cakes or muffins made with only beaten egg whites in the batter will fall like a failed soufflé. Make sure that you have at least one unbeaten egg white in the batter to hold the cake up.

Develop a "crust" on top

This is created by egg whites when the batter is beaten too much after the eggs are added. Actually, in creaming, volume is formed by beating the butter or the butter and sugar. Once you add the eggs, you do not increase the volume of the cake more by beating, but you can get this meringuelike crust. To avoid it, blend the eggs in on low speed until just incorporated, with a minimum of beating.

Too crumbly

Not enough gluten formed. Alter your mixing procedure so that some liquid and flour are combined before the flour and fat are mixed.

For information on cheesecakes, see the recipes in *BakeWise*, pages 333–34 and pages 341–43.

CHEESECAKES

See Chapter Two: Proteins, "Sweet and Savory Cheesecakes 101."

BISCUITS

For light, moist biscuits, a wet dough is the secret. My grand-mother's biscuits are a perfect example.

As a little girl, I followed my grandmother around the kitchen. For breakfast, lunch, and dinner, she made the lightest, most wonderful biscuits in the world. I used her bread bowl, her flour, her buttermilk—I did everything the same—

and I shaped the biscuits just like she did. But mine always turned out a dry, mealy mess. I would cry and say, "Nannie, what did I do wrong?" She was a very busy woman with all my uncles and grandfather to feed three meals a day, but she would lean down and give me a big hug and say, "Honey, I guess you forgot to add a touch of grace."

It took me twenty years to figure out what my grandmother was doing that I missed. I thought that the dough had to be dry enough to shape by hand. She actually had a very wet dough. She sprinkled flour from the front of an oblong wooden bowl shaped like a trough onto the top of the wet dough at the other end of the bowl, pinched off a biscuit-size piece of wet dough, and dipped it in the flour. She floured the outside of this wet dough so that she could handle it. In a hot oven, this wet dough creates steam to puff and make featherlight biscuits. Combing the wet dough with a low-protein flour like Tenda-Bake produces incredibly light, moist biscuits.

"TOUCH OF GRACE" BISCUITS

What This Recipe Shows

Self-rising flour provides even leavening and low protein for tenderness.

Wet dough provides more liquid for moisture and steam for lightness.

Nonstick spray

2 cups self-rising flour or low-protein Southern flour like
Tenda-Bake

¼ cup sugar

¾ teaspoon salt

¼ cup shortening

⅔ cup heavy cream

About ¾ cup buttermilk (see Note)

1 cup plain lower-protein flour (like bleached all-
purpose), for shaping

2 tablespoons butter, melted

NOTE: If you are not using low-protein Southern flour,
it will take more than 1 cup buttermilk.

Arrange a shelf slightly below the center of the oven and preheat the oven to 425°F (375°F if using a convection oven).
Spray an 8- or 9-inch cake pan with nonstick spray.

In a large bowl, stir together the self-rising flour, sugar, and
salt. Work the shortening in with your fingers until there are
no huge lumps. Gently stir in the cream. Stir in the buttermilk
until the dough resembles cottage cheese. It should be a sticky
mess—not soupy, but thick.

Spread the plain (not self-rising) flour out on a plate or pie
pan. With a medium ice cream scoop (about 2 inches or #30)
or large spoon, place 3 biscuit-size scoops of dough well apart
in the flour. Sprinkle flour over each. Flour your hands. Turn a
dough ball in the flour to coat, pick it up, and gently shape it
into a round, shaking off the excess flour as you work. Place
the biscuit into the prepared pan. Gently coat each dough ball

in this manner with flour and place the shaped biscuits in the pan smushed up against their neighbors. Continue scooping and shaping all the dough.

Bake the biscuits until they are lightly browned, 20 to 25 minutes. Brush with the melted butter. Invert the biscuits onto one plate, remove the pan, then invert them onto another plate so they are right-side up. With a knife or spatula, quickly cut between the biscuits to make them easy to separate and remove. Serve immediately. "Butter 'em while they're hot."

Makes 12 to 14 biscuits

COOKIES

Cookies are a microcosm of baking, in which the chemistry of each ingredient has a huge effect on the finished cookie. You make many decisions when deciding on a cookie recipe: which kind of flour, which fat, which sweetener, which leavener, whether to add liquid. Your choices determine if the cookie will be flat and crisp or soft and puffy, pale gold or deep brown.

Which Flour?

Higher-protein flours, such as bread flour or unbleached flour, can create more of the strong, elastic gluten that makes cookies chewy. If cookies are too crumbly, use bread flour and sprinkle it with a little water (to form gluten) before combining the flour with other ingredients. Cake flour and bleached all-purpose flour have lower-protein levels. If you prefer a tender cookie rather than a chewy one, choose one of these flours and mix the fat, sugar, and flour before you add any liquid. The amount of protein in the flour affects browning. The more protein in the flour, the browner the cookies. Cookies made with unbleached all-purpose flour or bread flour will be browner than those made with bleached all-purpose flour or cake flour. Low-protein cake flour is acidic, which reduces browning even more.

Higher-protein flours absorb more liquid, so cookies will spread slightly less as they bake than those made from the same recipe but using lower-protein flours. If your recipe uses cake flour and an egg, however, you'll get less spread, because the acidic flour makes the egg set fast.

Protein levels also affect a cookie's height. Lower-protein flours don't absorb as much water as high-protein flours, so they make more steam, which puffs cookies more.

Which Sugar?

Sugar type influences browning and texture. Corn syrup is mainly glucose—a sugar with a structure that makes it brown at a lower temperature than granulated sugar (sucrose). Cookies made with corn syrup will be browner. Sweeteners can make a cookie crisp or soft. Cookies made with sugars that are high in sucrose (such as granulated sugar and maple syrup) or glucose (such as corn syrup) tend to stay crisp. Sweeteners high in fructose (such as honey) act differently. Fructose is hydroscopic, meaning it absorbs water from the air, so cookies made with a lot of honey get soft upon standing. Brown sugar is more hydroscopic than granulated sugar. Brown sugar is also slightly acidic, so it can help limit spread in cookies made with an egg.

Butter?

Butter melts immediately in a hot oven, so cookies made with butter will spread more as they bake. (Also, butter is about 18 percent water, which contributes to spreading.) Shortening, on the other hand, melts at a higher temperature than butter, so cookies have more time to set in the oven and will stay domed.

The fat you use also makes a small difference in how brown your cookies will be. Since protein promotes browning, cookies made with shortening, which has no protein, will be slightly less brown than those made with butter, which has a little protein.

Baking Powder or Baking Soda?

Your choice of baking powder or baking soda affects color more than leavening. Baking powder contains baking soda and enough acid to neutralize the soda and doesn't influence the color of cookies. But baking soda by itself is alkaline and is a major contributor to browning. In most recipes, 1 teaspoon of baking powder or ¼ teaspoon of baking soda will leaven 1 cup of flour. When the leavening is more than this, the bubbles get big, rise to the surface, and pop, and there goes your leavening. In most cookie recipes, the amount of baking soda is greater than the amount actually needed for leavening and is used primarily for color.

Liquid?

More liquid means more spread, unless you use an egg. Many cookie recipes have no liquid, per se, but depend on the water in butter (which, again, contains about 18 percent water) to make enough gluten to hold the cookies together. Other recipes may use 1 or 2 tablespoons of liquid or an egg. The amount and type of liquid can influence the spread and puff of cookies.

Usually, the more liquid (if it isn't an egg), the more spreading. When an egg contributes the liquid, there's little tendency to spread. This is particularly true if there's an acidic ingredient (such as brown sugar, cake flour, or chocolate) in the dough, which makes the egg set quickly and limits spread. A bit of extra liquid, or the liquid from an egg, turns to steam and can make cookies puff more.

COOKIE PROBLEMS

Cookies stick to the pan

Cookies can become so cemented to a pan that you have to soak them off! Some cooks erroneously think not greasing the pan will prevent the cookies from spreading. The cookies spread because of the type of fat in the batter, or because the batter is too thin (see the above section "Liquid?"). Not greasing the pan will not solve this.

To prevent cookies from sticking, bake them on new release foil, silicone baking mats, parchment paper, or on a heavy cookie sheet sprayed with nonstick spray. Or you can use one of the heavy pans that do not stick made by USA Steel.

Cookies have a brief moment of perfect opportunity. When you first take them out of the oven, the cookies will tear apart if you try to remove them from the hot pan. After about 2 minutes, the cookies will have cooled enough to be removed perfectly intact, but after 10 minutes, they can become cemented to the pan.

Cookies spread too much

Too much free liquid; dough made with a fat with a sharp melting point like butter; too high a ratio of fat to flour. Since different flours absorb different amounts of water, high-protein flour like bread flour or unbleached flour will limit free liquid and limit spreading. Using a little shortening (a fat that remains the same texture over a range of temperatures) will limit spreading. If there is an egg in the recipe, you can incorporate an acidic ingredient like cake flour, brown sugar, sour cream, etc., which will cause the egg to set faster and limit spreading. The temperature of the cookie dough going into the oven has a minor effect on the spread, especially with all-butter cookies. A very cold dough will spread less.

Cookies are too pale or too dark

Protein and sugar in the dough determine the color of the baked cookies. For darker cookies, add more protein in the form of an egg or egg yolk, or switch to a higher-protein flour. Some sugars like glucose (corn syrup) enhance the browning reaction. Substituting even 1 tablespoon of corn syrup for the granulated sugar increases browning. For lighter cookies, cut the protein by eliminating egg and/or switch to a lower-protein flour like cake flour or White Lily, or use a mix of all-purpose flour and cake flour.

Also, acidity can make baked goods pale. Many cookie recipes contain more baking soda than is needed for leavening. It is there for browning.

Cookies crumble

They do not have enough gluten or protein to hold them together. For cookies without an egg, switch to a higher-protein flour like unbleached or bread flour, and sprinkle a tablespoon of water over the flour to form some gluten before adding the flour to the other ingredients. Little lumps will form, but have faith and continue on.

CHAPTER EIGHT

MORE DESSERTS

Here are more ways to be *Kitchen Wise* when it comes to sweets!

CRYSTALS

Crystals are an intimate part of our lives—from fragile patterns of ice on a windowpane to mighty glaciers to sparkling snow-white sugar and salt crystals.

Cooks need to be masters of crystals. Sometimes we need to prevent crystals from forming—for example, when making caramel—but many times we need to make not just crystals but special *types* of crystals. In making candies like fudge, divinity, taffy, and even pralines, we want tiny crystals to form so that the candies will be firm but smooth and creamy. When tempering chocolate, you need to get the cocoa butter to set in just the right crystalline structure to give the chocolate a firm, shiny surface. In ice cream, we need baby-fine crystals for that luscious, velvety-smooth, melting-in-your mouth sensation.

Crystals are the solid form of many substances. When molecules of an element or compound cool and slow down, they join together in a precise formal pattern unique to that substance. Each molecule must be in its exact right place for the crystal to form.

To get these precious crystals to form, we must have a very concentrated mixture of our substance—the molecules need to be packed together just ready to form crystals. The temperature must be low enough that the molecules are moving very slowly. Now, with packed-together, slow-moving molecules, we can make the substance crystallize just by stirring vigorously. When we stir, the molecules bang into each other and crystals start to form.

Candy

In candy making, we get our molecules squeezed close to each other by boiling off part of the liquid. How can we tell when we have boiled off enough water or concentrated the mixture enough?

Water boils around 212°F (this varies with altitude—water boils at lower temperatures at high altitudes). When there is a lot of water in our mixture, it boils around 212°F. When there is less water, the boiling point goes up. So, we can tell just by the temperature at which it boils how concentrated a mixture is.

Candy recipes tell us the temperature to heat the mixture to. If you make candy and it does not firm up—crystals do not form—it is probably because the mixture is not concentrated enough. Thermometers can be off as much as 10°F. Usually, if you simply boil the mixture to 3°F or 4°F higher than your first try, the candy will work.

When a mixture is very hot, its molecules move fast, but as it cools, the molecules slow down and it is easier for them to join together.

When we make candy, we get the mixture to the right temperature so that the molecules are concentrated and just ready to join together. If we shake the pan or even remove the thermometer, a few crystals form. As the mixture cools, these crystals grow and the candy becomes "grainy." On the other hand, if we let the mixture cool a little so the molecules have slowed down and it is just ready to crystallize, then when we stir vigorously, we get millions of baby crystals at once, and the candy is smooth and creamy.

When our mixture is concentrated and cooled a little, with the least little shake or stir, its molecules try to form crystals. Each molecule moves into its proper location and crystals form. But if we have a similar but slightly different sugar present, when one of its molecules moves into place, the crystal will not form since it's not the right sugar.

So, whenever we do not want crystals, all we have to do is add a similar but different sugar. When we make caramel and do not want crystals, we can add a little corn syrup (glucose, one of the two sugars that make up sucrose, table sugar).

Another way to prevent crystals is to add a mild acid like a few drops of lemon juice or vinegar or a pinch of cream of tartar. Acids break down some of the sucrose into glucose and fructose, so now we have three different sugars in the mixture and crystals will not form.

We actually have a lot of control using these similar but different sugars. With small amounts, we can slow down crystal formation, making many candies smoother. When small amounts of different sugars are present, we may have to take the mixture to a higher temperature for our candy to crystallize.

There are still other ways to make fine crystals. Things that coat baby crystals as they form, like egg white, gelatin, or pectin, work well to create smooth dishes. For example, the pectin in a tablespoon or two of preserves coats ice crystals as they form in ice cream, making it creamier.

Learning about crystals and controlling them give us a great appreciation of Mother Nature's wonderful ways.

ICE CREAM

Ice creams fall into two major categories. Philadelphia (also called New York, American, or plain) ice cream contains no eggs and is simply sweetened flavored cream lightened with milk and frozen. Ice cream made with eggs or egg yolks, usually in the form of a cooked custard base that may or may not include a little starch, is called French custard, or French custard ice cream.

Fine ice cream has a soft, light consistency, full body—not runny or spongy—and a creamy smoothness in the mouth. Both the ingredients and the techniques used have a hand in creating this wonderful mouthfeel. In addition to sugar, dairy products (especially milk fat and milk protein) play a major role in the texture of ice cream by helping limit crystal size and trap air bubbles. Stirring fine air bubbles into ice cream as it freezes lightens and softens ice cream.

SUGAR

The amount of sugar used has a major effect on ice cream's texture. When ice cream freezes, some of the liquid freezes into pure ice crystals. The liquid left behind becomes more and more concentrated. Since sugar lowers the freezing point of a liquid, as the liquid becomes more concentrated, its freezing point gets lower and lower, so that you have some portion of the ice cream left unfrozen at freezer temperature. For an ice cream soft enough to be scooped when it is removed from the freezer, the initial mixture has to have enough sugar to leave some liquid at freezer temperature. However, if there is too much sugar, your ice cream will be mush.

DAIRY PRODUCTS

All dairy products have several components that affect ice cream. Milk proteins and milk fat trap air when stirred, and the tiny air bubbles this creates lighten the mixture. Milk solids get in the way when ice crystals are trying to grow, effectively keeping them small. The fats in dairy products coat ice crystals and prevent them from enlarging. Fats also act as a lubricant, making even ice cream with larger crystals feel smooth on the tongue. Other components of dairy products lower the freezing point and thus help maintain the necessary unfrozen syrup between ice crystals, just as sugar does. These dairy products include calcium salts and other salts, as well as lactose, the form of sugar in milk. However, be aware that lactose is not as soluble as sucrose (table sugar); if there is too much lactose in cold ice cream, it will crystallize and cause the ice cream to feel sandy, with gritty crystals.

Different dairy products have varying amounts of these effective ingredients. For example, heavy cream has much more fat and less lactose than evaporated milk or condensed milk. Some ice creams contain some evaporated milk, but also some cream, so there is not an excessive amount of evaporated milk.

Heavy cream is a great multipurpose ingredient in ice cream. Cream is thicker than milk and has more fat clumps and is therefore much better at trapping and holding air when stirred. The high fat content of cream makes it very effective at limiting ice crystal size; it also acts as a lubricant between crystals. In addition, the fat helps cream hold air that was trapped when stirring. Cream has some of the milk solids that limit crystal size, and it has only a limited amount of lactose, which can cause grittiness.

Milk, on the other hand, has proteins to trap air when stirred, but does not have as much fat as cream and cannot hold air permanently as cream can. Milk does not have as much fat to help limit crystal size, but it does have more milk solids than cream, and these milk solids are even more effective than fat at controlling crystal size. Milk, with its lower fat content, does not give ice cream as smooth a mouthfeel as cream does, but it does contribute a lightness that you do not get with cream alone.

Condensed milk, evaporated milk, and powdered dry milk are major contributors of milk solids to help limit crystal size. However, all have a high concentration of lactose; if too much is used, lactose crystals form, and the result is an ice cream with a sandy texture.

PECTINS, GUMS, AND GELATIN

Pectins are huge molecules that grab water and form soft gels. Pectin, whether from fruit alone or from concentrate, is what makes jellies and jams set up. Pectin and/or gums and gelatin work in a similar way to help produce soft, smooth, creamy ice creams.

When ice is exposed to slightly higher temperatures (when you open the freezer door, for example), the small crystals melt. Ordinarily, when the ice gets cold again, this water freezes onto bigger crystals and enlarges them. This thawing and refreezing process creates the big crystals sometimes found on the surface of ice or ice cream in the freezer. Pectin keeps ice crystals small in two ways. First, due to the large size of its molecules, pectin gets in the way when ice crystals try to form and enlarge. Second, if a lot of pectin is present when small ice crystals melt, the pectin simply holds the water in a soft gel.

Beware when using pectin concentrate. With too much pectin (or gelatin or gums), the ice cream will set up like jelly and become a nonmelting solid. This destroys part of the sensuousness of ice cream—the sensation of cold melting to nothingness.

The addition of preserves is a great idea. They contain good concentrated flavor plus a small amount of pectin for creaminess. Preserves can be swapped with sugar tablespoon for tablespoon.

HONEY

Honey, like sugar, lowers the freezing point of water, so it can be used in place of some of the sugar in an ice cream. Because honey consists of sugars with smaller molecules than table sugar, it is more than twice as effective at lowering the freezing point as table sugar. Harold McGee recommends substituting 1 tablespoon of honey for 2½ tablespoons of sugar.

WINE AND LIQUEUR

Alcohol also lowers the freezing point of water, just as sugar does. Using alcohol gives you the advantage of using a little less sugar, or you can leave the sugar quantity the same and get a softer ice cream. A little liqueur is preferred to wine, because at freezing temperature, you get very little flavor from the wine.

CHOOSING THE BEST RECIPE

A recipe for ice cream can be as simple as sweetened cream lightened with a little milk. Ice cream and sherbet recipes are not as exacting as those for granitas and sorbets, since the dairy products are so effective at limiting crystal size and incorporating air. The milk proteins and heavy cream in ice cream and sherbet trap air bubbles as you stir them, and the fat, proteins, and calcium salts from the dairy products help the sugar control the number and size of the ice crystals.

A small amount of salt (about ⅛ teaspoon per batch of ice cream) is a vital contributor to flavor. It reduces bitterness to allow both the perception of sweetness and the flavor of the cream to come through. In French ice creams, egg yolks, the great emulsifiers, contribute silky smoothness.

Whether you are making Philadelphia or French ice cream, one step is essential for optimum smoothness if using any milk or half-and-half in the recipe. The milk or half-and-half should be heated to 175°F, just below scalding. I do not know the exact nature of the changes this heating causes—perhaps denaturing or partial coagulation of some of the proteins. Whatever it is, the effect is a noticeably smoother texture of the ice cream. It is not necessary to heat cream, which has very little protein.

AGING

After heating any form of milk (or half-and-half) in a recipe, and combining the ingredients, the mixture is allowed to "age" for 4 to 12 hours at a temperature between 32°F and 40°F. This is the usual refrigerator temperature. This aging before freezing improves the body and texture as well as the flavor of the ice cream. W. S. Arbuckle, an authority on commercial ice cream, strongly recommends aging 12 hours for rich ice creams.

FREEZING

The temperature of the mixture when it goes into the ice cream maker and the temperature of the freezing container itself determine how fast freezing takes place. With modern ice cream makers that have their own refrigeration units, and even with those in which you freeze the coolant overnight, the only control you have is the temperature of the mixture when it goes into the ice cream maker. A starting temperature between 27°F and 35°F works well. Below the lower temperature in that range, the mixture will freeze immediately, and you will get large pieces of ice. Above 45°F, you run the risk of the heavy cream being churned to butter.

Ice Cream Making at a Glance	
What to Do	Why
Include a small amount of salt in the recipe.	Salt enhances the flavor of the other ingredients.

What to Do	Why
If the ice cream is sandy or gritty on the tongue, reduce the amount of evaporated milk, powdered dry milk, or condensed milk in the recipe.	All have high lactose content and cause lactose crystals to form.
Heat any milk or half-and-half to 175°F.	For a smoth-textured ice cream.
Let the ice cream mixture "age" for 4 to 12 hours at 32°F to 40°F before freezing.	To improve body and texture of the ice cream.
Have the mixture between 27°F and 35°F when it goes into the ice cream maker.	To prevent the mixture from freezing too fast, which will produce large ice crystals and not incorporate air.
With hand-cranked ice cream makers, crank slowly at first.	To keep the temperature the same throughout the mixture.
With hand-cranked ice cream makers, crank faster when thickening and freezing begin.	To keep crystals small and beat air into the mixture.

CARAMEL

Caramel desserts are always popular. A little science can save you from disaster with caramel. To make caramel, you must boil off all the water and then melt the sugar and cook it until the wonderful brown caramel compounds form. If you stir while there is still water present, the sugar will crystallize out. Adding a similar but different sugar prevents this. So, the easy way to a successful caramel is to add some corn syrup (glucose) to your table sugar (sucrose). You can also add a mild acid, like a few drops of lemon juice or vinegar, which breaks some of the sucrose into glucose and fructose.

In 2010, I was honored to be invited to teach at the World Pastry Forum; I taught a three-hour class for five days. Chef Andrew Logan, known as Drew, assisted me and did demos, too. We had executive chefs from large hotels that served banquets for more than a thousand people and many teachers from chefs' schools—a prestigious group who deserved our best. Chef Drew did something wonderful with caramel that I had never seen before.

Normally, to make a caramel sauce, you make the caramel, heat heavy cream to a boil, and then, off the heat, with extreme care, keeping yourself way back, pour some of the hot cream into the caramel. The caramel is over 340°F and the heavy cream, even at a full boil, is only 212°F, so you have an explosion! Chefs always dread doing this and most of us have splatter burns on our arms from making caramel sauce.

Chef Drew said he was going to use gravity to make "safe caramel cream." He whipped cold heavy cream until it was about the thickness of a thick cream sauce. He placed the pan with the hot caramel on the counter and poured in about one-third of the cold whipped cream. No explosion! I couldn't believe it! Chef Drew explained that the cream was lighter because we had whipped it a little and it simply sat on top of the heavy hot caramel.

He let it just sit for about 1 minute, then he stirred gently with a whisk. It bubbled as the whisk incorporated the cream into the hot caramel, but it did not explode. He then added another third of the whipped cream and stirred, and finally added the last of the cream. He explained that he did not add the cold cream all at once to prevent the cold temperature from setting the caramel at the top rock hard. He had a beautiful creamy caramel. He heated it for a few minutes while stirring to get rid of any bubbles left from the whipped cream and finished it off with a little butter.

After all those years of dreading adding the cream to a caramel sauce, I just thought this was a miracle. I thought it was worth the cost of the trip for pastry chefs just to learn this. Chef Drew had generously shared his recipe. Now you, too, can make a safe caramel sauce.

ANDREW LOGAN'S SAFE CARAMEL CREAM

Here is a safe way to make a marvelous thick caramel cream. Chef Drew used his to fill thin chocolate shells to make perfect little candies, but it has many uses—thinned, it is a delicious caramel sauce.

What This Recipe Shows

Glucose prevents the caramel from crystallizing.

Whipping the cream lightens it so that it floats on top of the fiery-hot caramel to cover and cool.

½ cup (170 g) light corn syrup (Chef Drew used 150 g
Albert Uster Imports' Pastry Ideale Glucose Syrup)
1 cup (7 ounces/200 g) sugar
1⅓ cups (11 ounces/317 g) heavy cream, cold
2 tablespoons (1 ounce/29 g) butter

In a heavy saucepan, stir together the corn syrup and sugar. Cook over medium heat, without stirring, until you have a dark caramel. In a bowl, whip the cold cream to lighten until it is the consistency of a thick sauce. With the caramel off the heat, add the cream in thirds. After adding the first third, allow it to stand for 1 minute and then whisk the cream in thoroughly. Add the second third, whisking it in thoroughly, and then whisk in the final third. Allow to cool to 100°F, then beat in the butter with an immersion blender.

Let cool and pipe into small rectangular chocolate shells. This will fill about 100 small candies.

CHOCOLATE

WHAT IS CHOCOLATE?

To make chocolate, the shells and germs are removed from cocoa beans, which are then crushed, fermented, and roasted. The portion of the bean remaining, the cotyledon, is ground with or without sugar to produce a paste. This paste is kneaded (conched) to produce fine chocolate.

Chocolate is a mixture of finely ground cocoa particles in cocoa butter with or without sugar. Cocoa butter makes chocolate the sensual experience that it is. Cocoa butter has a sharp melting point, which is right at body temperature. You bite into hard, firm pieces of chocolate, then seconds later, your mouth is filled with aromatic, luxurious, thick liquid and the sublime taste of real chocolate.

Chocolates can vary in their amounts of cocoa particles, amounts of cocoa butter, amounts of sugar, and additives (emulsifiers, dairy products, flavorings like vanilla or vanillin).

Unsweetened Chocolate (Baking Chocolate)

The paste of cocoa butter and cocoa particles (chocolate liquor) is ground without sugar, with an emulsifier and possibly vanilla or vanillin, then tempered and cooled. In the US, this is baking chocolate.

Dark, Bittersweet, and Semisweet

By federal regulation, this chocolate must contain a minimum of 35 percent chocolate liquor. Until the past few years, top American and European brands contained 50 to 55 percent chocolate liquor, with the rest being sugar. This is the chocolate that we usually eat and use in cooking.

High-Percentage Chocolates

These are the new chocolates that contain 60 to 70 percent—or even more—chocolate liquor. They contain a lot more cocoa particles and a little more cocoa butter than regular semisweet and bittersweet chocolates. The older chocolates with 50 to 55 percent chocolate liquor contained 20 to 22 percent cocoa particles; now the chocolates with 60 to 70 percent chocolate liquor contain 28 to 30 percent cocoa particles. This makes a big difference in the amount of liquid we must use to blend these chocolates with other ingredients in recipes (see the section "Moisture: Seizing," below).

Couverture

This is fine chocolate that contains a larger amount of cocoa butter than regular semisweet or bittersweet chocolate. It is more free-flowing when melted. It is perfect for coating candy centers. Couverture chocolates can have the same amount of cocoa particles as regular semisweet or bittersweet chocolate, but they contain a lot more cocoa butter.

White Chocolate and White Confectionery Coating

White chocolate contains no chocolate liquor. It consists of cocoa butter, sugar, dairy products, and flavorings. The better brands contain cocoa butter, but others (called white confectionery coatings) are made with partially hydrogenated soy, palm, palm kernel, or cottonseed oil.

FDA standards require products to contain a minimum of 20 percent cocoa butter and a maximum of 55 percent sucrose (sugar) to be labeled white chocolate.

Milk Chocolate

In addition to sugar, this chocolate contains heavy cream or dairy products. You can see from the following chart of FDA standards that milk chocolate is required to have a minimum of 10 percent chocolate liquor. You will find that the flavors in milk chocolates vary greatly—some are creamy, while some are more caramelly.

FDA Standards of Identities for Cocoa-Derived Products	
Product	% Chocolate Liquor
Chocolate liquor	100
Bittersweet and semisweet	35
Sweet (like German's)	10 to 35
Milk	10 (minimum)
White	0

COOKING WITH CHOCOLATE

You can have glistening, thick melted chocolate and suddenly, just a few degrees hotter, you have dark, grainy lumps in pale, golden oil. Or, even more startling, your shiny melted chocolate can suddenly become a dull, solid, grainy mass. These two most common problems with chocolate—separation and seizing—are caused by overheating and by moisture.

Overheating: When Melting Chocolate Separates

Chocolate is a complex mixture of particles and fats. When heated, the fats soften, melt, and become more fluid as heating continues. Finally, at a little over 120°F, the fats separate from the particles. As heating continues, the particles lump together in dark black knots that settle to the bottom. The fats are now a pale, golden liquid. This separation of chocolate with heat is an irreversible happening.

This separation temperature, 120°F for dark chocolate and 115°F for lighter chocolates, is not very hot. Experienced chocolatiers are very careful not to exceed these temperatures. Ideally, to melt chocolate, chop it into small pieces or process it in a food processor for a few seconds. These fine pieces melt faster and more evenly than large lumps. Stir chocolate constantly while melting to keep the temperature even throughout. Chocolate can be safely melted in many different ways: on very low heat or over hot—not simmering—water, or in the microwave at 50 percent power for semisweet or 30 percent for milk or white chocolate, stirring every 15 seconds. Heat and stir until the chocolate is just melted.

To prevent irreversible separation, the chocolate must not get over 120°F. Most thermometers are off by as much as 10°F. Your own body temperature of 98.6°F is your best gauge. If you touch a dab of melted chocolate just above your upper lip (a very sensitive area) and it feels cool, you know it is below 98.6°F. All the chocolate will be melted and it will feel warm but not really hot to your upper lip at 120°F.

Moisture: Seizing

Even the tiniest bit of moisture—even steam—can cause flowing, shiny melted chocolate to become a solid, dull mass. Dr. Richard Schwartz at Wilbur Chocolates explains this with a sugar bowl example: If you pour a cup of boiling water into a sugar bowl, it dissolves all the sugar—no lumps. But if you dip the spoon that you just used to stir your coffee into the sugar bowl, you get little grainy lumps of sugar. The moisture from your spoon causes the dry sugar particles to glue together.

This is exactly what happens when you get a little moisture in chocolate: the fine, dry sugar and the cocoa particles glue together to change melted chocolate into a solid, dull mass. If chocolate seizes, is there anything you can do to rescue it? Yes and no. You can apply the sugar bowl example and add a little more water so that all the particles get wet and no longer stick together. Work a tablespoon of warm water into the grainy mess. When this is incorporated, work in another tablespoon until you have a smooth, shiny chocolate again. This slightly watered-down chocolate is fine for many uses—icing, fillings, etc.—but will not work for enrobing, where you need a hard finished product.

Understanding seizing means several things to the cook. First, avoid any situation in which you have a small amount of liquid with chocolate. The minimum amount of liquid needed to prevent seizing is 1 tablespoon per 2 ounces of chocolate. Any recipe with less liquid than this will not work. Unfortunately, there are truffle recipes that instruct adding a small amount of liqueur to melted chocolate, which will cause it to seize.

The cook has a fail-safe way to avoid seizing. Why melt chocolate alone and risk seizing when you combine it with other ingredients? Just melt it with liquid from the recipe and totally avoid the problem. As long as you have the magic 1 tablespoon liquid per 2 ounces chocolate, it will not seize. You will notice that experienced dessert cooks write their recipes in just this way—melting the chocolate with liquid from the recipe. Maida Heatter melts chocolate and butter together in her Palm Beach Brownies. Alice Medrich melts chocolate, butter, and corn syrup together for her glassy-smooth chocolate icing. Ortrud Carstens melts chocolate with hot cream for ganache.

A GRAY COATING FORMS
ON THE SURFACE OF THE CHOCOLATE

If chocolate is not tightly wrapped, moisture from the atmosphere condenses on the surface when the temperature lowers. This moisture dissolves some sugar from the chocolate. When the air warms again, the moisture evaporates, leaving behind a gray film of very fine sugar called a sugar bloom.

If chocolate is stored for six months or more at a temperature in the high seventies, tiny amounts of some fats in the cocoa butter melt and float to the surface of the chocolate, forming a gray film called a fat bloom. Fat blooms and sugar blooms look alike, but there is a slightly oily feel to fat bloom.

GANACHE—A CHOCOHOLIC'S LIFELINE

Ganache is made of chocolate and cream—a heavenly combination. Ganache can turn into icings, truffles, soufflés, even tortes, to name a few. Classically, cooks make three forms of ganache: soft ganache (two parts cream to one part chocolate by weight), medium ganache (equal weights of cream and chocolate), and firm ganache (one part cream to two parts chocolate by weight).

Soft Ganache

Soft ganache can be chilled and whipped like whipped cream to create fabulous chocolate mousses—elegant, luscious desserts. Soft ganache mousses can be used as cake fillings or as parts of impressive creations. You can make "chocolate whipped cream" mousses with bittersweet, semisweet, or white chocolate ganache.

Medium and Firm Ganache

Both medium and firm ganaches can be used as icing for cakes. In my favorite ganache icing, I use a ratio of cream to chocolate that produces a ganache halfway between medium and firm.

Firm ganache can become truffles (as in the recipe that follows) or a torte with the addition of eggs. Sherry Yard has a wonderful recipe for Baked Whisky Tortes using a firm ganache in her book *The Secrets of Baking*.

THE SMOOTHEST-EVER AMARETTO TRUFFLES

10 ounces semisweet chocolate, broken into 1-inch
    pieces
6 ounces milk chocolate, broken into 1-inch pieces
5 tablespoons butter, cut into tablespoon-size pieces
¼ cup heavy cream
4 egg yolks, lightly beaten
¼ cup amaretto liqueur
2 cups tempered melted chocolate (see the section
    "Tempering" below)

In a food processor, chop the semisweet and milk chocolates together until the texture of a fine grate.

In a 9- to 10-inch skillet, melt the butter over medium heat. Remove from the heat and stir in the cream and egg yolks. Return the mixture to a low heat and cook, stirring constantly

---

by scraping the bottom with a wide spatula, until tiny bubbles form around the edges and you see a wisp of steam rising from the surface. Remove from the heat and continue to stir. Add the chopped chocolates and the liqueur. Stir gently until all the chocolate has melted and the mixture is smooth. You may need to return the skillet to low heat for several brief periods, stirring constantly, to melt all the chocolate.

Place the skillet in the refrigerator to cool the chocolate. When the chocolate is partially set, remove it from the refrigerator. With a large melon baller, a tiny ice cream scoop, or a spoon, shape the chocolate into 1½-inch balls and set them on a tray lined with wax paper. Allow them to stand at room temperature for about 30 minutes, then dip them one at a time into the tempered melted chocolate to coat. Place them on a piece of foil and allow them to stand until cool and set.

When the coated truffles are firm, refrigerate them until shortly before serving. Serve in little fluted candy cups. Store any leftover truffles in the refrigerator.

Makes about thirty 1½-inch truffles

OTHER INGREDIENTS
IN GANACHE CREATIONS

Any time you want a soft shine, such as with a ganache icing, think corn syrup. As my friend Harold McGee puts it, "Corn syrup is a liquid that attracts water and fills in spaces between fine sugar particles to produce a glass-smooth surface." Using corn syrup in a ganache gives a deep shine to the dark surface.

I used to think that ganache icings had to be nothing but

cream and chocolate, but then I read Sherry Yard's work. (She was formerly the executive pastry chef at Spago.) In her ganache glaze, she adds apricot jelly, which sweetens and adds subtle flavors and a little pectin to slightly firm the glaze. What a great idea!

GANACHE TECHNIQUES

The classic method of preparing ganache is to place chopped chocolate in a heatproof bowl, bring heavy cream to a boil, pour the hot cream over the chocolate, and stir rapidly together until it is smooth. I know that this method has been passed down for generations, but it can have problems.

If the cream and chocolate are not successfully combined, the ganache can separate and form an oily, shiny glaze on top, or it can contain hard little undissolved chocolate specks. These are two separate problems. The oil on top occurs when an emulsion (a mixture of two liquids that ordinarily do not go together, like fat and water) breaks and the liquids start to separate. The undissolved chocolate specks are what chefs call "seizing." It is this seizing that I think can be a problem when pouring the hot cream over the chocolate. Young pastry chefs are taught to approach ganache worrying about an emulsion, but it is seizing that I am always concerned about. Having too little water-type liquid and too many cocoa particles, even for a split second, can create hard little chocolate specks.

In seizing, beautiful, satiny, flowing melted chocolate can suddenly become a rock-hard, grainy mass. Chocolate is composed of fine, dry particles (cocoa and sugar) in rich fat (cocoa butter). In melted chocolate, a few drops of water, or even steam, can cause these dry particles to stick together (the sugar bowl analogy in the section "Cooking with Chocolate: Moisture: Seizing" illustrates this).

There is plenty of water-type liquid in heavy cream to prevent the cocoa particles from gluing together (seizing), but if the liquid is added to the chocolate, there can be a split second when there are many dry cocoa particles and too little liquid, so tiny stuck-together particles can form. I feel it is much safer to add the chocolate to the cream (as I do in my recipes for Simple Chocolate Mousse and Shiny Ganache Glaze in *BakeWise*).

As long as the chocolate is finely chopped, the temperature is hot enough to melt the chocolate, and the ganache is stirred, I have not seen problems with the ganache breaking, but I have seen problems with chocolate specks even with experts.

In a tiny kitchen in Erice, Italy, I watched as a French restaurant owner/chef poured boiling cream over chopped chocolate while a famous French pastry chef stirred the mixture vigorously. The pastry chef got a product that he was unhappy with two out of five times. He pointed out the tiniest chocolate specks in the otherwise smooth mixture. There were only the three of us in the kitchen; the two chefs spoke little or no English, and I spoke no French, so I could not ask my questions or suggest something to try. And after all, this was one of the most famous pastry chefs in France. I remained respectfully silent.

A reasonably fail-safe procedure for adding the hot cream to the chocolate is by using a food processor: Put the finely chopped chocolate in the food processor. With the processor running, pour the boiling cream down the feed tube onto the chocolate and process until combined and smooth. Alice Medrich does caution that this should take no longer than 15 seconds. You need to get the liquid in very quickly.

TEMPERING

Cocoa butter, the fat in chocolate, can crystallize in any one of six different forms (or polymorphs, as they are called). Unfortunately, only one of these, the beta crystal (or Form V), hardens into the firm, shiny chocolate that cooks want. Form VI is also a stable, hard crystal, but only small amounts of it form from the good beta (Form V) crystals upon lengthy standing. When you buy commercial chocolate, it is in the form of beta crystals.

When you melt chocolate and heat it to above 94°F, you melt these much-desired beta crystals, and other types of crystals can set up. If you simply let melted chocolate cool, it will set up in a dull, soft, splotchy, disgusting-looking form. Even the taste is different. Fine chocolate has a snap when you break it and a totally different mouthfeel from the other cocoa butter forms.

How can we get chocolate to set up in these hard, shiny beta crystals? The process of melting chocolate and then cooling it so that it will form beta crystals is called tempering. Tempering is necessary only for real chocolate, which contains cocoa butter, not for compound chocolate or summer coating, which contains fats other than cocoa butter.

You need a truly accurate thermometer when tempering chocolate. Most kitchen thermometers (even the instant-read digital type) can be off by as much as 10°F. If you do much chocolate work, you'll want a laboratory-quality thermometer.

When I asked chocolate expert Dr. Paul Dimick about tempering, he said the easy way out is to never heat chocolate over 91°F to 92°F. Beta crystals do not melt until 94°F.

By staying below 92°F, you never lose all those prized crystals, and your melted chocolate is already tempered. What a wonderful idea!

Your goal is to barely melt the chocolate. All these crystals have a range over which they melt, and chocolate melts at 89°F to 90°F, even though all the beta crystals do not melt until heated to above 94°F. You can keep the chocolate over a very low heat source (like a heating pad) and, with constant stirring, melt two-thirds of it. Then remove it from the heat and patiently continue stirring until all the chocolate has melted. For dark chocolate, ideally you want to end up with a temperature of 89°F to 91°F (87°F to 89°F for milk chocolate or white chocolate). If you have kept the chocolate below 92°F during all this, it is still tempered and ready for use. Cocoa is primarily produced in two manners; one is plain cocoa like Hershey's and the other is called Dutch, which has been alkaline processed.

COCOA PROBLEMS

A baked product with cocoa is dry

Cocoa powder, because of its starch, acts like flour in a recipe. Reduce the amount of flour in the recipe in the same amount as the cocoa, or add liquid to compensate for the additional starch.

Too much spread, or slow setting

Dutch-process cocoa powder is alkaline, and will change the acidity of a batter. This will cause more spreading in cookies and will slow the setting of cakes or muffins as they bake. Acids make proteins set faster, so a slightly acidic batter is important in the setting or cooking of proteins. A more acidic cookie batter will not spread as much, acidic muffin batters produce muffins that "peak" better, and a little vinegar in a pie crust makes it set a little faster. Any time you need chocolate to set fast, such as in high-altitude baking, you do not want to use Dutch-process cocoa powder.

Dish containing cocoa and uncooked egg yolks (possibly chocolate mousse) thins in the refrigerator

Alpha-amylase, an enzyme in the egg yolks, destroys the starch gel formed by starch in the cocoa powder (which contributes to the thickening of the mousse), just as uncooked egg yolks thin starch-thickened custards. Heat after adding the egg yolks to kill this enzyme.

Flavor Not Intense Enough

More-intense chocolate flavor can be obtained from cocoa powder by pouring a small amount of boiling water over the cocoa.

CONCLUSION

With your new knowledge from *KitchenWise*, you should now know how to spot bad recipes, and how to fix them.

You should know how to solve common cooking problems from tough meats to stuck cookies.

You should know how to keep your vegetables a brilliant green, how to keep red vegetables red, how to preserve nutrients in vegetables, and how to maintain the shape of cooked fruits and vegetables.

You should know how to make smooth, creamy sauces and know which starch to use to preserve the clarity of bright-colored fruit and which to use in dishes that will be frozen.

You should know how to create outstanding dishes from magnificent, moist cakes to flavorful, light bread to juicy meats to the perfect chocolate dessert with a magnificent, deep, shiny glaze.

In brief, you should be a great cook!

FOOD SAFETY BASICS

We in the United States are fortunate to have probably the most abundant and safest food supply in the world thanks to our agricultural and animal husbandry expertise and our food overseers like the USDA, the FDA, and the CDC.

Keeping food safe in the kitchen is an important part of preventing food-borne illness. The USDA in its excellent publication "Keep Food Safe! Food Safety Basics" * identifies four basic guidelines for food safety:

- Clean—Wash hands and surfaces often
- Separate—Don't cross-contaminate
- Cook—Cook to proper temperatures, checking with a food thermometer
- Chill—Refrigerate promptly

It covers all the basics in a simple, easy-to-read way: shopping, storage, thawing, preparation, cooking, serving, leftovers, refreezing, and a cold storage chart. The guidelines are simple and have some interesting science behind them.

---

* https://www.fsis.usda.gov/wps/portal/fsis/topics/food-safety-education
/get-answers/food-safety-fact-sheets/safe-food-handling/keep-food-safe
-food-safety-basics/CT_Index

SHOPPING

The USDA has three shopping tips: buy refrigerated or frozen food after nonperishables; don't buy food past the sell-by date; and never choose meat or poultry in torn or leaking packaging.

These shopping tips help avoid food-borne disease by keeping food at safe temperatures, buying food that is fresh, and avoiding cross-contamination.

These are important because many different types of microorganisms can grow on food, for example yeasts, molds, bacteria, and viruses. Some bacteria, like salmonella and listeria, are killed in cooking. Some bacteria, like E. coli and botulinum, produce toxins that may not be killed in cooking. Viruses are in raw or undercooked shellfish. Also some parasites can affect fish, meats, and other food. A cook's main defense is not to allow conditions that can produce these toxins by following proper food safety procedures from the grocery store to the dinner table.

When food is in the "danger zone," above 40°F and below 140°F, bacteria grows twice as fast as other times, doubling in twenty minutes. Many of the USDA food safety regulations are focused on minimizing the time food is in the danger zone and/or keeping it out of the danger zone altogether. For example, buying refrigerated and frozen foods last helps minimizes their time in the danger zone.

Buying well-sealed meat or poultry (and putting it in a separate produce bag) prevents cross-contamination due to leaking bacteria-filled raw meat juices.

Ideally when shopping carry an insulated chest with ice or a freezer bag with a freezer pack in your car and place fish, meat, and poultry in a large leakproof plastic bag or bags in the chest. Place milk, yogurt, cheese, and food to be eaten uncooked in a separate area of the cooler or in a separate cooler bag. If you are going to be out long, carry a separate chest for fruits and vegetables.

STORAGE

For storage, the goal is again to keep food out of the danger zone and to avoid cross-contamination. The USDA recommends that the refrigerator be kept at 40°F or below and the freezer at 0°F or below. Keep a thermometer in the refrigerator to check the temperature. All perishable food should be refrigerated within two hours of purchase. Then, poultry, fish, ground meats, and variety meats should be cooked or frozen within two days of purchase, and beef, veal, lamb, or pork within three to five days.

You need to overwrap when freezing because grocery store wrap on fresh meat is permeable to allow oxygen to maintain the bright red color (oxymyoglobin). This is why grocery wrap will not prevent meat from drying out, so, for freezing, meat should be wrapped in nonpermeable plastic wrap, like Saran, or in products clearly labelled "freezer," or well wrapped in freezer paper, which has a plastic barrier. Heavy-duty foil is also an option.

Chicken, fish, and ground meat keep for only two days in the refrigerator, while beef, lamb, and pork keep for three to five days, before needing to be cooked or frozen. Large pieces of meat keep better than ground meats because ground meats have a huge surface area that could have been exposed to bacteria, going through the grinder or just being in the air. Seafood is highly perishable because its enzymes are accustomed to working in cold water, a low-temperature environment. Therefore home refrigerators do not slow down spoilage in fish as they do other meats. Seafood should be used at once. If you have to keep seafood for a day or two, the following may help keep it fresh: Spread the seafood over the bottom of a large clean strainer and pile ice on top of it. Place the strainer in a bowl that is deep enough so any liquid will be well below the bottom of the strainer. This setup keeps the fish very cold and also as the ice melts the liquid rinses the bacteria off the seafood. Since the wash is away from the seafood, it cannot recontaminate the fish as it could if the fish were packed on ice.

Where is the best place in the refrigerator to store meat and other foods? The temperature in the refrigerator varies in different locations, with the back and bottom rack typically being the coldest since cold air sinks and repeated opening of the door to the refrigerator warms the front. Meat keeps best at 28°F to 32°F, which is colder than most home refrigerators. Some refrigerators have a meat compartment, which is set to several degrees colder than other parts of the refrigerator. If you don't have this, you can check the temperature in your refrigerator with a refrigerator thermometer and you can even try to set your refrigerator so the back will be closer to 32°F. Just make sure it won't freeze your vegetables and other more tender food in the other parts of the refrigerator, and that meat is well wrapped and below any cooked food, so raw meat juices cannot drip on any food.

Dairy foods should be kept toward the back of the refrigerator, higher up, well away from raw meat and unwashed produce. Raw eggs should be kept away from ready-to-eat food and away from raw meat.

The USDA gives inputs on canned food storage as well. High-acid canned foods can be stored for twelve to fifteen months. Low-acid foods keep two to five years if the can is unopened, in good condition, and has been stored in a cool, clean, dry place. Discard cans that are dented, leaking, bulging, or rusted. It is not just fresh meat that can harbor very dangerous bacteria and toxins, but canned goods as well, one example being clostridium botulinum, which produces botulism. Cooking will not destroy botulism, so throw the can out.

THAWING

The USDA gives three options for thawing frozen foods. The refrigerator allows slow, safe thawing—just make sure thawing meat and poultry juices don't drop into other food. For faster thawing, place food in a leak-proof plastic bag, submerge in cold tap water, and change the water every thirty minutes. For fastest thawing, use the microwave. When food is above 40°F and below 140°F ("the danger zone") bacterial growth is encouraged. One goal when thawing foods is to minimize bacterial growth. Thawing in the refrigerator is safest since it keeps food below 40°F. However, neither of the other two methods guarantees that the food temperature will stay below 40°F. Therefore, when using those other two methods, cook the food immediately after thawing to minimize time in the danger zone.

PREPARATION

For food preparation, the USDA recommends always washing hands with soap and water for twenty seconds before and after food preparation. Don't cross-contaminate. Keep raw meat, poultry, fish, and their juices away from other food. Use separate cutting boards for meats and vegetables. After cutting raw meat, wash your hands, cutting board, knife, and counter with hot soapy water. Marinate meat and poultry in covered dishes or in plastic freezer bags in the refrigerator to safely contain raw meat juices. Sanitize all cutting boards in 1 tablespoon liquid bleach and 1 gallon of water. Even in spotless kitchens cross-contamination can occur.

Immediately wash anything that comes into contact with raw meat. If you use a dishcloth to wipe a knife that was just used to cut raw chicken and later use that towel to dry a plate, you have just spread bacteria from the raw food to the plate.

Vegetables and fruit can also contain bacteria. Wash vegetables under running water, before peeling or cutting, to avoid getting surface bacteria on the knife and into the interior of the fruit or vegetable, especially if it will be eaten raw.

COOKING

Cook all raw beef, pork, lamb and veal steaks, chops, and roasts to a minimum internal temperature of 145°F, and allow the meat to rest for three minutes before carving or consuming. The USDA adds that for reasons of personal preference, consumers may choose to cook meat to higher temperatures. Note, the rest period is needed to ensure that pathogens are killed as the meat will often continue to cook during the rest period.

All raw ground beef, pork, lamb, and veal are to be cooked to an internal temperature of 160°F as measured with a food thermometer. This is higher than the USDA temperature for the steaks, chops, and roasts because the interiors of these cuts of meat have not been touched by anything or exposed to air, so that limits the amount of bacteria that can be present in the interior of the meat.

The FDA's Food Code for restaurants is also instructive. For example, tenderizing chops or steaks by sticking a fork-like tenderizer into the meat or injecting anything into the meat will expose the inside of the meat to bacteria. In such cases, the Food Code specifies cooking the meat to a higher temperature.

The USDA specifies that poultry should be cooked to an internal temperature of 165°F, as at this temperature salmonella is destroyed as well as campylobacter bacteria and avian influenza viruses.

To minimize the amount of time food is in the danger zone when cooking, the USDA recommends using an oven temperature no lower than 325 degrees when roasting meat and poultry.

The USDA guidelines on food safety are excellent guidelines for cooks and help protect the public from food-borne illness. The USFDA's Food Code also gives technical safety guidelines for food service industries. Both the USDA and the USFDA generally agree on minimum safe cooking temperatures and that eating undercooked meat poses health risks. However, because the USFDA guidelines are for food service industries, there are some differences due to equipment, sourcing of meat, and type of customers or audience.

The USFDA's Food Code specifies that for roasts only, where the meat meets guidelines for extra safe production, with specialty equipment, certain bacteria can be killed by holding *all* parts of the meat at lower temperatures for longer times. Another example of this idea is pasteurization when salmonella is killed by holding eggs at 140°F for three and a half minutes.

The Food Code specifies that a restaurant that serves a highly susceptible population as a general clientele may not serve undercooked meat of any kind. A highly susceptible population includes, for example, those with weakened immunity and the very young and the very old.

The only meat that can be served to the general population (not the "highly susceptible") undercooked is whole-muscle, intact beef steak, which is made less of a risk because of the quality of the meat, and because the top and bottom outer surfaces, where most bacteria are, are cooked to 145°F or above, with color change on all surfaces. It is still considered a risk, however. Some obstetricians recommend that expectant mothers not eat undercooked beef steak.

Anything else must either carry a warning so the customer knows eating the food poses a risk, or the establishment must provide proof of the safety of the preparation. This is how some restaurants serve steak tartare and ceviche. Again, these are still considered a risk and so cannot be served if the restaurant serves a highly susceptible population as a general clientele.

Ceviche is an example of using an acid, rather than heat, to cook meat. Lime juice is used, which is much more acidic than lemon juice. Many bacteria and parasites will not be killed by the lime juice, so the fish must be frozen first for a week at –4°F (which is colder than most home freezers) to kill parasites. Care must still be taken to avoid bacteria that is not killed by freezing.

It is safer to cook meat to or beyond the temperature guidelines specified by the USDA (home) and Food Code (restaurant). There are a few areas where people do not cook food to these guidelines, for example, poached eggs and rare and medium-rare steaks. For poached eggs, or anywhere raw egg yolks or whites (as in some meringues) are required in a recipe, it is safer to use pasteurized eggs. Pasteurized eggs have been heated to kill bacteria and can be used for at-risk populations. There are some other methods of preparing safe egg yolks and whites. See my book *CookWise*, pages 195–96. However, because of the possibility of cross-contamination, these methods should still be used with care, so pasteurized eggs cooked well done may be the safer choice for those at risk.

Cheeses can also have issues for at-risk populations. High-risk groups such as pregnant women, newborns, older adults, and people with weak immune systems due to cancer treatments, AIDS, diabetes, or kidney disease should not eat feta, Brie, Camembert, blue-veined cheeses (such as Gorgonzola), or Mexican-style soft cheeses such as queso blanco or queso fresco *unless labeled pasteurized.* This is because foods containing *Listeria monocytogenes* can cause very serious illness, especially for high-risk groups.

Steak, an intact whole muscle cut, can be surface treated to reduce bacteria. Apparently it is harder for parasites to penetrate the dense meat of beef so the risk is more on the outside of the beef, which can be cooked, reducing the risk. Pork, on the other hand, is more susceptible to parasites that infect the flesh, such as trichinosis or worm cysts. While production methods for farm-raised pork have improved in the United

265

States to help lessen this risk, wild game carries a greater risk and should be handled accordingly. The conditions in which the animal was raised also affect the quality of the meat and the amount of bacteria parasites in the meat. So, while rare or undercooked beef may be less risky to eat than undercooked chicken or pork, it can still carry toxoplasmosis and so should not be eaten by at-risk populations. The safest thing to do is to meet or exceed the USDA guidelines for cooking.

SERVING

The USDA guidelines help keep food out of the 40°F to 140°F danger zone. Hot food should be held at 140°F or warmer. Cold food should be held at 40°F or colder. When serving food at a buffet, keep hot food hot with chafing dishes, slow cookers, and warming trays. Keep cold food cold by nesting dishes in bowls of ice, or use small serving trays and replace them often. Use a food thermometer to check hot and cold holding temperatures. Perishable food should not be left out more than two hours at room temperature, and only one hour when the temperature is above 90°F.

LEFTOVERS

The USDA recommends discarding any food left out at room temperature for more than two hours, or one hour if the room temperature was above 90°F. Other food should be placed in shallow containers and immediately put in the refrigerator or freezer for rapid cooling. Use most cooked leftovers within three to four days and reheat leftovers to 165°F.

For leftovers, and for cooling off food just made to be refrigerated, don't put too much hot or warm food in the refrigerator. Take care not to put warm leftovers right next to or on the shelf just below or above raw meat or dairy. That could raise the temperature of the meat or dairy into the danger zone above 40°F, spoiling the meat or dairy. Also, remember never to put cooked food below raw meat, so raw meat juices can't drip on cooked food. An ice bath for food to be added to the refrigerator will cool it off before and/or when putting it in the refrigerator. Date leftovers so they can be discarded if not used within three to four days. Leftovers should be reheated to 165°F to account for possible additional bacterial growth while they were sitting out.

REFREEZING

Food thawed safely below 40°F in the refrigerator may be refrozen before cooking, while food thawed by the water or microwave methods must be cooked immediately.

REFRIGERATOR AND FREEZER STORAGE CHART

The USDA has a very useful chart showing storage times for the refrigerator and the freezer. Freezer storage times are for quality only. Refrigerator storage times help determine how long before a food must be eaten, frozen, or tossed. Use an appliance thermometer to monitor storage temperatures in the refrigerator and freezer.

One thing to note, freezing at 0°F or below will not kill bacteria. It will become dormant and will still require cooking to be killed. Some toxins produced by bacteria cannot be killed by cooking. Part of the defense against this is not to allow conditions that encourage bacterial growth in the first place and to follow food safety guidelines. Also, while freezing to −4°F for seven days will kill many parasites in fish, this may not kill all parasites if the fish is too thick.

One reason quality may suffer in the freezer is the development of off flavors in meat because fat continues to oxidize even while frozen. Saturated fat fares better in the freezer than unsaturated fat. So beef, veal, and lamb last in the freezer longer than seafood, chicken, and pork.

Following the USDA's simple food safety procedures and some of the tips added here from the grocery store to the dinner table will help keep your food safe.

ACKNOWLEDGMENTS

My gratitude and thanks to:

Kara Watson, editor extraordinaire, and her team. This book would not have been possible without Kara, from naming it to amazing editing, Kara does not remove your work. She understands it and makes suggestions to greatly enhance it.

Erich Hobbing for his outstanding design of *BakeWise* and *KitchenWise*.

My gratitude to the whole staff at Simon & Schuster who worked on my book. Thank you for your wonderful and greatly appreciated contributions.

Terry Infantino and Sherry Hecht, my precious daughters, whose tender loving care made it possible for me to finish this book and whose expertise and knowledge were invaluable in the editing.

Judith Weber, an outstanding agent with invaluable knowledge of publishers and editors who finds ideal situations for her clients. She found the perfect editor for me.

Dr. Harold McGee, author of *On Food and Cooking* and *The Curious Cook* and my hero and beloved friend who has always been there for me, whether it is a food question or an editing problem.

Bob and Francine Schwartz for help in reviewing and encouragement during the writing of this book, for their expert advice in marketing, and for the wonderful dinners we enjoyed together.

Jaddie Dodd, with his computer expertise, gave me immediate help whenever I called.

Doris Koplin for many wonderful years of teaching together and sharing knowledge.

Gena Berry, a wonderful cook, caterer, and consultant who produced my DVD *Shirley O. Corriher's Kitchen Secrets Revealed!* and who has been a constant inspiration.

To the University of Wisconsin–Stout and UNC Greensboro. I appreciate your using my DVD and work in your schools to train upcoming generations of cooks.

Houston and Mary Smith for their reviewing, encouragement, and suggestions during the writing of *KitchenWise*.

Nathalie Dupree, a great teacher and food writer who gave me a firm culinary background.

Dr. Robert Shewfelt, Professor Emeritus of Food Sciences and Technology, University of Georgia; Dr. Carl Hoseney, Emeritus Professor, Grain and Science Industry, Kansas State University; Dr. Ing C. Peng from Purdue University; Dr. Estes Reynolds at the University of Georgia; and Elmer Cooper, chemist, Red Star Yeast: experts in their fields who graciously and kindly shared their time when I called with questions.

INDEX

Index

Index

Index

Index

Index

Index

Index